Sailmaker
Plus

Alan Spence
with Jane Cooper

HODDER
GIBSON
PART OF HACHETTE UK

The Publishers would like to thank the following for permission to reproduce copyright material:

Photo credits Page 1 © Bob Thomas/Getty Images; page 5 © Hulton-Deutsch Collection/Corbis; page 65 © Hulton Archive/Getty Images; page 66 © Hulton-Deutsch Collection/Corbis; page 69 (top) © Anthony Ling/Alamy; page 69 (bottom) © Dave King/Dorling Kindersley/Getty Images; Page 71 (top) © John Springer Collection/Corbis; page 71 (bottom) © David Moir/Reuters/Corbis; page 72 © PA Photos; page 73 © Robert James/Hodder Gibson; page 74 © Popperfoto/Getty Images; page 75 © Michael Ochs Archives/Corbis.

Acknowledgements 'Its Colours They are Fine' Reproduced with permission of Curtis Brown Group Ltd, London on behalf of Alan Spence. Copyright © Alan Spence 1977.

Every effort has been made to trace all copyright holders, but if any have been inadvertently overlooked the Publishers will be pleased to make the necessary arrangements at the first opportunity.

Although every effort has been made to ensure that website addresses are correct at time of going to press, Hodder Gibson cannot be held responsible for the content of any website mentioned in this book. It is sometimes possible to find a relocated web page by typing in the address of the home page for a website in the URL window of your browser.

Hachette UK's policy is to use papers that are natural, renewable and recyclable products and made from wood grown in sustainable forests. The logging and manufacturing processes are expected to conform to the environmental regulations of the country of origin.

Orders: please contact Bookpoint Ltd, 130 Park Drive, Abingdon, Oxon OX14 4SE. Telephone: (44) 01235 827720. Fax: (44) 01235 400454. Lines are open 9.00–5.00, Monday to Saturday, with a 24-hour message answering service. Visit our website at www.hoddereducation.co.uk. Hodder Gibson can be contacted direct on: Tel: 0141 848 1609; Fax: 0141 889 6315; email: hoddergibson@hodder.co.uk

© Alan Spence and Jane Cooper 2008
First published in 2008 by
Hodder Gibson, an imprint of Hodder Education,
Part of Hachette UK,
2a Christie Street
Paisley PA1 1NB

Impression number   7

Year   2014

Cover photo © Mary Evans Picture Library/Alamy
Illustrations by Charon Tec Ltd. (A Macmillan Company).

Typeset in 10.5/13 Stone Serif by Charon Tec Ltd. (A Macmillan Company).
Printed and bound by CPI Group (UK) Ltd, Croydon, CR0 4YY

A catalogue record for this title is available from the British Library

ISBN-13: 978 0 340 97303 5

CONTENTS

Activities and Assessment

The book you are holding is from the 4th printing (or later) of this title, where references to Standard Grade and Intermediate have been replaced by National 5. Additionally, some activities and comments/advice sections have been amended to make them appropriate for National 5 study.

Introduction

Sailmaker is set in the 1960s and was written in the 1980s. Here, Alan Spence explains how the play came to life.

How did the play come into being in the first place?

This goes back to the early 1980s. I had published a book of short stories called *Its Colours They Are Fine*. At that point STV wanted to make some short TV plays by Scottish writers. I wrote a 30-minute play called *The Palace*, adapted from part of a short story I'd written. It got good reviews and was later adapted to be a short stage play which was seen by Peter Lichtenfels of the Traverse Theatre in Edinburgh.

He got in touch with me about writing a full-length stage play. I revisited another short story I'd written called 'Sailmaker'. I could see how I could open it out. I took bits from another couple of my short stories including one called 'Blue' and over a few months came up with this play.

What were you trying to achieve with the play? What ideas did you want to explore?

When I write I don't start off with ideas or with trying to communicate anything. I just try to create something satisfying.

It's about trying to be true to my own experience and after that maybe touching on something that's deeper and more universal.

How much did you draw on events in your own life as you wrote the play?

The central relationship between the father and son is absolutely, directly autobiographical. My mother did die when I was 11 and my father did go though that whole spell of not being able to cope.

Something like the incident when the father is beaten up by the bookmaker did happen. My father had got involved with some money lenders and he got beaten up on the way home from his work one time. There was all of that going on and it filtered into my awareness.

Did your dad know that you'd written about the two of you in this way?

I wrote the play the year after my father died and I don't think I could have written it while he was still alive. I think it would have been too painful to sit and watch it together. He did read the short story 'Sailmaker' and he was OK with that, but the play goes into much more detail and more depth. I think that would have been hard for him to sit through.

The drama of the play is the boy getting older and coming of age and moving on out of the limitations of his background. He gets an education and eventually goes to university. At the same time for Davie, the father, his possibilities are closing down and he's declining. It's quite poignant how their two lives cross over.

What was it like when you saw events from your own life on stage like this?

I remember sitting in rehearsals one day watching the two actors playing the father and son. I was getting really exasperated with the boy and thinking, 'Can't he see that his old man is just doing his best?' I'd become detached enough to see them as characters. Then it was like a little light coming on in my head and realising that when I was Alec's age I couldn't see that either. Maybe the play was me coming to terms with my father and being more sympathetic to him.

How much are the other characters based on real people?

Billy and Ian are based on several different people. My father had a couple of brothers and possibly some elements of their personalities found their way into the character of Billy. I think that's something that writers do, they'll invent characters that have a bit of one and a bit of another and a wee bit that's just invented.

Sailmaker is over 30 years old now. How well do you think it has stood the test of time? What do you still like about it?

I'm pleased that it's still in print, still being read, still performed. I like the fact it's realistic. It's about actual events and the actual difficulties people had living in that kind of poverty. Overlaying that I think there's something poetic that comes through in the language, for instance in the monologue in the last scene when the boy talks about them burning the yacht. There's literal truth but there's also a poetic truth, a spiritual truth behind all that.

If someone has read Sailmaker and enjoyed it, which of your books would you recommend them to read next?

I wrote a novel called *Way To Go* that picks up on some of the themes in the play but it takes them much wider. The main character in the book goes to India and America and travels all over the place. It's quite funny too. Readers might like its black humour.

Context for

Sailmaker

SCENE

The setting of the play alternates between a Glasgow tenement flat (room and kitchen) and its surrounding streets and back courts.

The play begins in the early 1960s and continues through that decade.

This play was first performed at the Traverse Theatre Club, Edinburgh, on 29 April 1982.

Sailmaker

by
Alan Spence

ACT ONE

Dark. Light on ALEC, *centre stage.*

ALEC: Sometimes I wake up in the middle of the night and I can remember it. The feeling.

I was only a boy. Eleven.

There was this knock at the door. The middle of the night.

Batter. Batter.

It was a policeman. He said my mother had taken a turn for the worse. My father had to go down to the hospital.

I couldn't get back to sleep.

It was getting light by the time he came back . . .

(Lights fade up. DAVIE *enters, stands behind* ALEC*)*

DAVIE: Ah've got a bit of bad news for ye son. Yer mammy's dead.

ALEC: Part of me already knew, accepted it. Part of me couldn't. Part of me cried.

DAVIE: Ah've got a bit of bad news for ye son.

ALEC: I cried and a numbness came on me, shielding me from the real pain.

DAVIE: Yer mammy's dead.

ALEC: I was standing there, crying – real big deep sobs. But the other part of me, the part that accepted, was just watching.

DAVIE: Ah've got a bit of bad news for ye son.

ALEC: I was watching myself crying, watching my puny grief from somewhere above it all. I was me and I was not-me.

DAVIE: Yer mammy's dead.

*(*ALEC *turns to face him)*

There's just you an me now son. We'll have tae make the best of it. *(Turns away)*

Ah'll make some breakfast.

ALEC: Ah'm no really very hungry.

DAVIE: Naw. Ah'll make a cuppa tea.

(*Moves back, quietly busies himself, sets fire in hearth*)

ALEC: Later on I opened the window and looked out across the back courts. The breeze was warm. Everything was the same. It was very ordinary. Nothing had changed. I don't know what I had expected. A sign. Jesus to come walking across the back and tell me everything was all right. A window in the sky to open and God to lean out and say my mother had arrived safe. The sun shone on the grey tenements, on the railings and the middens, on the dustbins and the spilled ashes. It glinted on windows and on bits of broken glass. It was like something I remembered, something from a dream. Across the back, a wee boy was standing, blowing on a mouth-organ, playing the same two notes over and over again.

(*Two notes on mouth-organ, repeated, continuing while he talks*)

My mother was dead.

My mother was dead.

The breeze touched my cheek. It scattered the ashes round the midden. It ruffled the clothes of the wee boy standing there, playing his two notes.

Over and over and over.

I looked up at the sky, the clouds moving across. Just for a minute a gap opened up, a wee patch of clear blue.

(*Two notes continuing, then fade*)

DAVIE: We better get this place tidied up a bit son. Folk'll be comin back after the funeral.

(*Moves around as he is talking – ALEC remains static*)

As long as ye keep movin it doesnae hit ye. Get the fire goin clean the windaes dust the furniture think about somethin for eating don't stop keep yerself goin. Sometimes for whole minutes ye can nearly *nearly* forget

7

about it, shove it tae the back ae yer mind. Then maybe yer lookin for somethin and ye turn round tae ask her where it is an ye wonder for a minute where she's got tae and ye think maybe she's through in the room an ye catch yerself thinkin it and it hits ye an ye think Christ this is it this is me for the rest ae ma days.

ALEC: After the funeral. Back hame. House full ae people. Aunties an Uncles. Folk we hadnae seen for years. On and on and on.

DAVIE: That's it. They're aw away. Just you an me now son.

ALEC: Aye.

DAVIE: God, Ah'm shattered.

Isn't it funny the words ye use tae describe things. Shattered! (*Looking round.*) Place is in a right mess, eh? Still. Never mind. We can clear it up in the mornin, eh? Ach aye.

In the mornin. (*Exit*)

(*Lights up.* IAN *enters, running*)

ALEC: Ah had a yacht. Y'ought tae see it. (*Runs out for yacht*)

IAN: Put it in the canal. Ye can all see it.

ALEC: (*Comes back with yacht*) There!

IAN: Is that it?

ALEC: Aye. Ah found it in the Glory Hole.

IAN: (*Takes yacht, examines it*) It's got nae sails or nae mast or nothin.

ALEC: (*Takes yacht back*) Ah'm gonnae get ma da tae fix it up. Ma da's a sailmaker.

IAN: Your da sells stuff on the never never and collects the money roon the doors. He's a tick man.

ALEC: He's workin as a tick man. But he's really a sailmaker. That's his *real* job. That's his trade.

IAN: How come he disnae work at it?

ALEC: Don't know. Maybe there's nae jobs.

IAN: Ye need a trade. That's what ma da says. He's gonnae get me in wi him at the paintin when ah'm auld enough.

ALEC: Maybe ma da'll go back tae his trade. (*Holds up yacht*) That was a great poem he made up.

IAN: Your da?

ALEC: (*Nods*) Ah had a yacht

Y'ought tae see it

IAN: Your da didnae write that!

ALEC: Aye he did!

IAN: He didnae!

ALEC: He did!

IAN: Well how come ah've heard it?

ALEC: Maybe ma da told your da.

IAN: Aye, Maybc! (*Sarcastic*)

ALEC: Ye know, they must have had sailmakers away way way back in the aulden days, when there wis pirates an explorers an that. Right back . . .

IAN: Roman Galleys . . .

ALEC: Vikings!

IAN: When's yer da gonnae fix it up?

ALEC: Soon.

IAN: Ah can just see it. It would look great wi red sails. Just like the song.

ALEC: Eh?

IAN: There's a record. Red sails in the sunset.

ALEC: That's right, ah've heard it.

IAN: It's great. (*Sings*) Red sails in the sunset.

ALEC: (*Joining in*) Way out on the sea (*waves boat up and down in time. They laugh, self-conscious. ALEC brings boat down to rest on floor, face down.*)

ALEC: Used to be Jacky's. Ah got it when he went tae America.

IAN: Aw his stuff got shared oot. Ah got his soldiers.

ALEC: Did ye?

IAN: He's ma cousin tae, ye know. You're no the only wan!

ALEC: Must be great in America, eh?

IAN: Cowboys and gangsters an that.

ALEC: Magic.

IAN: Hey look, it's a submarine. (*Pushes yacht forward*) German battleship on the port bow. Prepare to torpedo.

ALEC: They're firing depth charges! Dive! Dive! Dive!

(IAN *makes explosion noises, 'blows up' yacht*)

ALEC: (*Taking yacht again*) It's a shark. It's gonnae get ye! (*Attacks* IAN *with it, going for his throat*)

IAN: Aaaaaargh!

(*They lose interest in the game*)

Hey, have you got any new comics tae swop?

ALEC: Ah got some in a parcel fae Jacky, but ah don't want tae swop them.

IAN: How no?

ALEC: They're real American wans. They're coloured. Ah don't want tae swop them for scabby auld black and white things.

IAN: But Jacky sent me some tae. We could just dae a straight swop.

ALEC: What've ye got?

IAN: Superman. Blackhawk.

ALEC: Ah've got some Superman as well. An a coupla Batman. An a Creepy Worlds.

IAN: Yer on!

ALEC: After tea?

IAN: Right!

(*They spit on their palms and shake hands, clinching the deal*)

ALEC: Ma da's quite late. Maybe he's gettin fish suppers for the tea.

IAN: Fish suppers? In the middle of the week?

ALEC: He's no very good at cookin.

IAN: Oh aye.

ALEC: Hey! Ah've got some great new foties for ma Rangers scrapbook. (*Shows* IAN *book*)

IAN: Where d'ye get the big coloured wan ae the team?

ALEC: In the Rangers handbook. It's a beauty, eh?

IAN: Brilliant.

ALEC: Blue really is the best colour.

IAN: That's what ma da says. He says it's God's favourite colour! Cause the sky's blue, and that's where God lives.

ALEC: Sea's blue as well. Look, ye even get blue in the fire – see thae blue flames there! Pity the grass is green.

IAN: But ye can get blue grass.

ALEC: Can ye?

IAN: They've got it in America. There's a group called Johnny Duncan and the Bluegrass Boys. They dae sorta country and western.

ALEC: That's right, (*Sings*)

Last train to San Fernando

Last train to San Fernando

IAN: (*Joins in*)

If you miss this one

You'll never get another one

Beedi Beedi Bum Bum

To San Fernando

ALEC: Hey, they should get some ae that blue grass for Ibrox!

IAN: Can ye imagine it!

ALEC: Ah've got somethin else ah wanted tae show ye. It's blue as well.

IAN: (*Looks at what* ALEC *has in his hand and recoils*) It's a holy medal!

ALEC: Our Lady.

IAN: Whit ye daein wi that?

ALEC: Ah found it.

IAN: Whit did ye keep it for?

ALEC: A just sorta . . . liked it.

IAN: Ye should fling it away. It'll bring ye bad luck.

ALEC: The middle part's blue . . . see. That's the colour ae Mary, the mother ae God.

IAN: How d'ye know that?

ALEC: Maureen told me.

IAN: (*Knowing*) Oh aye! So that's it, eh?

ALEC: What?

IAN: Ye've got a fancy for wee Maureen!

ALEC: Ah just . . . like her.

IAN: Next thing ye'll be carryin a rosary and crossin yerself!

ALEC: Don't be stupid! (IAN *laughs,* ALEC *shuts scrapbook, turns away*)

IAN: Hey c'mon! Don't take the huff! (*Coaxing*) Hey, what are we gonnae sing at the Lifeboys concert?

ALEC: Don't know.

IAN: How about that wan we were singin? Last train to San Fernando.

ALEC: Don't really know it. Just the chorus.

IAN: Me tae.

How about Singing the Blues? Ye must know that.

ALEC: Aye.

IAN: An blue's yer favourite colour, right?

ALEC: Aye. Funny how blue means sad, intit. It's no really a sad song but.

IAN: (*Sings*)

Ah never felt more like singin the blues

Cos I never thought that I'd ever lose

Your love babe

You got me singing the blues

ALEC: Ah never felt more like cryin all night

Cos everythin's wrong an nothin is right

Without you

You got me singin the blues

(*Sing together*)

The moon and stars no longer shine

The dream is gone I thought was mine

There's nothin left for me to do

But cry-y-y-y over you

ALEC: Ah'll tell ye somethin. It's a secret but. Don't tell anybody.

IAN: Awright.

ALEC: Promise?

IAN: Cross ma heart.

ALEC: It was after ma mammy died. Ah was lookin at the sky above oor hoose. An ah thought ah saw her.

IAN: Yer Ma?

ALEC: Mary. Our Lady. Dressed aw in blue, Ah couldnae be sure. But ah thought it was.

IAN: Above your hoose?

ALEC: Just for a second.

IAN: That's creepy. Did ye have that medal wi ye?

ALEC: Aye.

IAN: Maybe that's what did it. Put the idea intae yer heid.

ALEC: Maybe.

IAN: Ma da says when he dies he's gonnae get his ashes scattered on the pitch at Ibrox.

(*Both half-smile*)

ALEC: Show ye somethin else. (*Goes to glory hole, comes back with canvas bag, holds up shell*) This used tae be ma mammy's.

IAN: Some size eh. (*Takes shell*) Imagine the size ae the whelk ye'd get out ae that!

ALEC: Ah hate whelks.

(IAN *mimics picking out giant whelk, wriggling it, eating it. ALEC snatches shell back*)

If ye listen ye can hear the sea. (*Holds shell to his ear, then passes it back to* IAN)

IAN: (*Holding shell to ear*) So ye can. Wonder what sea it is?

ALEC: The Pacific. Naw, the Indian Ocean. (*Holds up shell*) Amazin colours. It's like . . . when the light shines on a patch ae oil on the street.

(*Takes out sheet of cellophane*) See this?

IAN: Cellophane.

ALEC: My ma used tae bring it hame when she worked in the bakery. Sheets an sheets ae it. They used it for wrappin cakes. Look . . . What colour is it?

IAN: Gold.

ALEC: Right. Watch! (*Opens it out*) Da raaa! See! It's clear. See right through it. Fold it up tight. (*Folds*) An it's gold again.

IAN: Aye right enough. Ah've noticed that.

ALEC: Wonder how it works. Where the colour goes.

Did ah ever show ye ma da's sailmakin tools?

IAN: Naw,

ALEC: (*Shows* IAN *tools*) These are called marlinspikes. Great name, eh?

IAN: (*Takes marlinspike, weighs it in his hand*)

Make a great chib!

ALEC: (*Takes another marlinspike from bag*)

Fence ye

(*They cross swords, fence with much clashing of blades*)

Swine!

IAN: Dog!

ALEC: Scurvy knave! Ah'll have ye keel-hauled!

IAN: Fifty lashes!

ALEC: Clap ye in irons!

IAN: Make ye walk the plank!

(*They continue fencing,* DAVIE *enters*)

DAVIE: Boys! Boys! Ye'll poke each other's eyes oot!

(*Last clash of blades, then they stop*)

Right. That's better. (*Looks at tools*) Where did ye get these anyway?

ALEC: In the Glory Hole.

IAN: Ah better be goin in for ma tea.

ALEC: Don't forget the comics.

(*Sees* IAN *out*)

DAVIE: (*Picks up tools*)

Marlinspikes.

ALEC: (*Coming over*)

You've been drinkin. Ah can smell it.

DAVIE: (*Breathes at him*) Just wan, son. Honest! Wee half at the end ae the day. Just helps me tae unwind. Up an doon stairs aw day, knockin folk's doors. Half ae them hide when they hear ye comin. Shove the light aff, shoosh the weans. (*Whispers*) Sssshhh! It's the tick man! Ah don't know.

(*Holds wooden fid in hand*) This is a fid. Made fae lignum vitae. Hardest wood in the world. Used it for splicin rope.

ALEC: What's this! (*Holds up leather palm*)

DAVIE: It's a palm. For shovin needles through the canvas.

ALEC: Ah was kiddin on it was a sorta glove. For fightin.

DAVIE: (*Laughs*) Knuckleduster!

ALEC: How come ye chucked yer trade?

DAVIE: *It* chucked *me*! The chandlers ah worked for shut doon. Ah got laid off. That was it. Nothin else doin. Nae work. Naebody needs sailmakers these days.

ALEC: (*Holds up yacht*) Could ye make me a sail for this? Ah found it in the Glory Hole tae. Ah thought you could fix it up.

DAVIE: Oh aye. It's a beauty, eh? Be nice, aw rigged out.

Can sail it in the park.

Course, it'll take time. Materials'll be dear. But ah'll see what ah can do.

ALEC: When?

DAVIE: Wait an see. (*Hands back yacht*) Who knows? Maybe ma coupon'll come up this week!

ALEC: Remember the last time ye won?

DAVIE: First dividend. Two quid!

Ah didnae let it go tae ma head mind! Didnae chuck ma job. Didnae buy a villa in the south of France. Ah think every second game was a draw that week! Never mind. Some ae these days.

(DAVIE *sits down, takes newspaper and scrap of paper from his briefcase, writes*)

Ah didnae bring in anythin for the tea. D'ye fancy nippin doon tae the chippy, gettin a coupla fish suppers?

ALEC: Awright.

(DAVIE *hands him money*)

Can ah get a pickle?

DAVIE: Get anythin ye like. Here's somethin else ye can do for me.

Themorra at dinnertime. Take this line tae the bookie.

ALEC: Och da!

DAVIE: Whit's the matter?

ALEC: It's just that . . . ah don't *like* that bookie. He's creepy.

DAVIE: Away ye go!

ALEC: An that back close where he has his pitch is aw horrible an smelly.

DAVIE: (*Waves his line*) But this could be worth a fortune! Three doubles, a treble, an accumulator. If it comes up we're laughin.

Here son, ah'll leave it here wi the money inside it.

ALEC: (*Picks up line, reads it*) Why d'ye always write Mainsail at the bottom ae yer line?

DAVIE: That's what ye call a nom-de-plume. The bettin's illegal ye see. The bookie gets done fae time tae time. An if you put yer real name on the line, the polis might book you as well. So ye use a made-up name.

ALEC: Mainsail

(*Pockets line*)

(ALEC *comes forward,* IAN *enters with football which he passes to* ALEC)

IAN: A wee game!

ALEC: Heidy fitba!

IAN: Right, ah'm Rangers. You can be Celtic.

ALEC: You're always Rangers!

IAN: It's ma baw isn't it.

ALEC: Ah'm no goin Celtic. Ah'll be . . . Real Madrid.

IAN: Suit yerself. Ah'll still beat ye!

(*They play, heading and kicking the ball back and forth*)

ALEC: Aw shite! Ah just remembered.

IAN: Whit!

ALEC: Ah'm supposed tae take ma da's line doon tae the bookie.
Comin wi me?

IAN: Aye, awright.

(*They walk*)

ALEC: Ah hate gawn.

IAN: How?

ALEC: Don't know. Ah just don't like the bookie. See when ah was dead wee, ah used to hear ma da talkin aboot the bookie, only ah didnae know what it meant, an ah thought he wis saying boogie.

IAN: Like the boogies ye pick oot yer nose?

ALEC: Aye!

(*They laugh*)

IAN: Whit did ye think he wis, a wee guy covered in snotters?!

(*Wails, waves his hands towards* ALEC)

The boogie man's gonnae get ye!

ALEC: That's the thing tae. They were always tellin me tae watch out or the bogie man would get me. An ah must've got the two things mixed up.

IAN: Daftie!

ALEC: Tell ye somethin else ah thought as well. When ma da used tae talk aboot tryin the pools, ah always imagined him fishin in these big deep pools a watter.

IAN: Fishin!

ALEC: Aye.

IAN: Whit a diddy!

ALEC: Ah'm talkin aboot when ah wis wee!

IAN: (*Laughs*) Bogeymen an pools a watter!

ALEC: Cannae tell you anythin!

(*Turns away*)

IAN: C'mon, ah'll race ye!

(*They turn, skid to a halt*)

Is this the close?

ALEC: Ye can tell by the smell!

Make sure ah've got the line.

IAN: The fishin line!

(ALEC *swipes at him, he dodges back*)

Watch out for the bogie man! He'll shove ye in the pool!

(ALEC *chases him offstage*)

(*Enter* DAVIE *and* BILLY, *talking as they walk*)

DAVIE: Eh, Billy . . . that coupla quid ah tapped off ye. Could it wait till next week?

BILLY: Aye sure.

DAVIE: Things are still a wee bit tight.

BILLY: What's the score?

DAVIE: Eh?

BILLY: Ye shouldnae be this skint. What is it?

DAVIE: Ah told ye. It's the job. Just hasnae been so great. No sellin enough. No collectin enough. No gettin much over the basic.

BILLY: Aye, but ye should be able tae get by. Just the two ae ye.

DAVIE: It's no easy.

BILLY: Ye bevvyin?

DAVIE: Just a wee half when ah finish ma work. An by Christ ah need it.

BILLY: Ye bettin too heavy? Is that it?

DAVIE: (*Hesitates then decides to tell him*) It started a coupla months ago. Backed a favourite. Absolute surefire certainty. Couldnae lose. But it was even money, so ah had tae put quite a whack on it. (*Slightly shamefaced*) Best part ae a week's wages.

BILLY: An it got beat?

DAVIE: Out the park. So ah made it up by borrowin off the bookie. He does his moneylender on the side. Charges interest.

BILLY: An every week ye miss the interest goes up.

DAVIE: This is it. Now when ah pay him ah'm just clearin the interest. Ah'm no even touchin the original amount ah borrowed. Ah must've paid him back two or three times over, an ah still owe him the full whack.

BILLY: Bastard, eh? Sicken ye. *And* he's a pape.

(DAVIE *laughs*)

DAVIE: Still, Aw ah need's a wee turn. Ah mean ma luck's got tae change sometime hasn't it? Law of averages.

BILLY: Whatever that is.

DAVIE: Things have got tae get better.

BILLY: It's a mug's game. The punter canny win.

DAVIE: Got tae keep tryin.

BILLY: Flingin it away!

Look, Don't get me wrong. Ah don't mind helpin ye out, but ah'm no exactly rollin in it maself.

DAVIE: You'll get yer money back.

BILLY: That's no what ah mean!

DAVIE: What am ah supposed tae dae? Get a job as a company director or somethin! Ah'll go doon tae the broo in the mornin!

BILLY: There must be some way tae get this bookie aff yer back for a start.

DAVIE: Aye sure!

BILLY: Ah mean, you've *paid* him.

DAVIE: Ah knew his terms.

BILLY: It's no even legal.

DAVIE: Neither is gettin his heavies tae kick folk's heids in.

BILLY: So maybe he's no the only wan that knows a few hard men.

DAVIE: (*Sighs*) What a carry on, eh?

BILLY: Hey. Remember when we were wee, we used to fight like cat an dog?

DAVIE: Ah could beat ye an all!

BILLY: Oh aye, ye were too fast for me. Quick on yer feet. The old one-two. Ma only chance was tae get ye in a bearhug.

DAVIE: Ah've still got the bruises!

BILLY: Ah remember one time we were havin a right old barney, an da was tryin tae sleep – must've been on the nightshift. An he came runnin out the room in his shirt-tail an clattered the pair ae us!

DAVIE: He was a tough auld customer right enough. Had tae be in these days.

BILLY: D'ye know he *walked* fae Campbeltown tae Glasgow tae get a start in the yards! Tellin ye, we don't know we're livin.

Ah hear the boy's daein well at school.

DAVIE: Oh aye. He's clever. He'll get on.

BILLY: He'll get on a lot better if you screw the heid, right?

DAVIE: C'mon Billy, ah dae ma best. It's just . . .

BILLY: Ah know it's hard on yer own an that . . .

DAVIE: Naw ye don't know. Naebody knows, unless they've been through it. (*Quieter*) Comin hame's the worst. The boy's oot playin. Hoose is empty. Gets on top of ye.

The other night there, ah got this queer feelin. Ah felt as if aw the furniture and eyerythin was *watching* me. Sounds daft, eh? Maybe ah'm goin aff ma heid!

BILLY: Bound tae take a while tae get over it.

DAVIE: If ah ever dae.

(*They cross to where* ALEC *is playing with yacht*)

BILLY: (To ALEC) How ye doin wee yin? What's this ye've got? (*Picks up yacht*)

ALEC: Used tae be Jacky's.

DAVIE: Ah'm gonnae fix it up, when ah've got the time.

ALEC: Ye've been sayin that for weeks!

BILLY: Ah could paint it if ye like.

ALEC: Would ye?

BILLY: Aye, sure. Should come up really nice. Ah'll take it away wi me. Get it done this week.

ALEC: This week!

BILLY: Nae bother.

ALEC: What colours will ye make it?

BILLY: Ah think the hull has tae be white. Ah've got a nice white gloss at work. The keel ah could dae in blue. Maybe put a wee blue rim round the edge here. An ah think ah've got a light brown that would do just fine for the deck. That suit ye awright?

ALEC: Great!

BILLY: Ye won't even recognise it. It'll be like a brand new boat.

ALEC: It'll be dead real, eh?

BILLY: It'll be that real we can aw sail away in it!

DAVIE: Away tae Never Never Land!

BILLY: Right, ah'll be seein ye.

(Takes yacht, exits)

(ALEC *follows him seeing him out, then comes back*)

ALEC: Uncle Billy's great isn't he.

DAVIE: Ach aye. Mind you, he's pure mental when it comes tae Rangers an aw that. Big Orange headbanger. But yer right. Underneath it he's a good lad. Solid.

(ALEC *gets ready to go, puts leather palm on hand, tucks marlinspike under his belt*)

Where ye goin?

ALEC: Out tae play wi Ian. See you later.

(*Comes forward,* IAN *enters carrying four lengths of bamboo cane*)

IAN: Ah've got the string an the bits ae cane.

ALEC: Great! Have ye got the hacksaw blade?

IAN: Aye. Have you got the tape?

ALEC: Aye.

IAN: Right. You make the bows an ah'll make the arras. D'ye know how tae dae it?

ALEC: Aye.

IAN: Ye pit a wee notch at baith ends, for the string. Then ye wind a wee bit tape roon, so the cane disnae split . . .

ALEC: Ah know! (*Sets to work, notches ends*)

IAN: Hurry up wi the blade. Ah need it.

ALEC: Whit fur?

IAN: Ye've got tae cut through the cane. If ye just break it in two, it aw splits, just makes a mess. (*Takes blade and saws*)

ALEC: Terrible noise it makes.

IAN: Sets yer teeth on edge.

ALEC: Like polystyrene when ye rub it on the windae. Like the teacher's chalk when it scrapes on the blackboard . . .

IAN: Don't talk aboot school. Ah hate it! Hey, comin we'll no bother goin back on Monday? We'll just run away and dog it forever!

ALEC: That would be brilliant! Where could we go?

IAN: We could go tae America and live wi *real* Indians. Jacky would help us.

ALEC: Ach, there's nae real Indians left. They aw get pit oot in daft wee reservations.

IAN: How aboot India then? Or Africa? We could live in a tree hoose.

ALEC: Pick bananas an oranges.

IAN: Hunt animals.

ALEC: Make pals wi some ae them but. Lions an tigers an that.

IAN: Make pals wi the darkies tae.

ALEC: Great white chiefs.

IAN: (*Beating chest*) Me chief Ian!

ALEC: We'd have tae gie wursels better names but.

IAN: Walla Walla Wooski!

ALEC: We could paint wursels tae. Wear feathers an bones.

IAN: Imagine bein cannibals. We could just eat white men that got lost in the jungle.

ALEC: Fancy goin intae the chippy an askin for two single fish an a whiteman supper!

IAN: Sausage rolls wi pricks in them!

ALEC: That's horrible!

IAN: Imagine fat Louie cuttin people up for pies!

ALEC: Like Sweeney Todd.

IAN: People are supposed tae taste like pork.

ALEC: Think ah'll stop eatin meat.

IAN: Ach don't be daft!

(*While talking, they have been carrying on with their work*)

ALEC: (*Flexing bow*) There!

IAN: (*Holds up arrows*) Right!

(ALEC *passes bow to* IAN, *who fires arrow*)

IAN: It's a goodyin.

ALEC: Gie me a shot.

(*Takes bow, fires low shot*)

C'mon we'll go huntin!

(*They exit*)

(DAVIE *in chair.* BILLY *enters, carrying yacht in bag*)

BILLY: Hey Davie, ah brought ye a coupla cowboy books. Ah know ye go in for the highbrow stuff. Dickens an that. But these are a good read.

DAVIE: Och naw. Ah'll read anything. Shane. That's a goodyin. Saw the picture.

BILLY: Alan Ladd, eh? Great stuff. Terrific.

(*Enter* ALEC)

There yar then! (*Holds out yacht*)

ALEC: Look at that! It's just like new.

BILLY: What did ah tell ye?

DAVIE: Ye did a nice job Billy. It's beautiful.

ALEC: Brilliant. (*Holds yacht, amazed*)

BILLY: Blue an white. Best colours in the world.

ALEC: Blue's ma favourite colour.

BILLY: There yar! The boy's got sense!

ALEC: Orange is good as well, isn't it?

BILLY: Orange is *great*!

ALEC: How about purple?

BILLY: Oh aye, purple's good.

ALEC: Red?

BILLY: Red's fine. So's yellow.

ALEC: Black an white?

BILLY: They're OK. They're no exactly good an they're no exactly bad.

They're sorta . . . nothingy.

But there's one colour we havenae mentioned, an that's the worst ae the lot, an that's . . . green! Ye don't like green do ye?

ALEC: No really.

BILLY: Terrible colour.

DAVIE: Away ye go! How can a colour be bad? Just because Catholics wear it.

BILLY: It's maybe no bad in itself, but they Catholics have *made* it bad.

DAVIE: Even Rangers play on green grass!

BILLY: Aye, they trample it under their feet!

DAVIE: It takes a green stem tae haud up an orange lily!

BILLY: Aye, well. The exception proves the rule, doesn't it!

DAVIE: (*Tuts*) Ach! Fillin the boy's head wi rubbish.

BILLY: (*To* ALEC) Anyway, there's yer yacht. An blue and white it is!

ALEC: (*To* DAVIE) Now will ye fix it up?

DAVIE: Be a shame not to. (*Crouches down*) Need to bring the mainmast up about here. Drill a wee hole in the deck, fit it in. Fix on a bowsprit for the jib, bring out a boom for the mainsail. Can work out the length an get dowelling cut to size. Taper it. Then there's the riggin, an material for the sails . . .

ALEC: Red!

BILLY: That'll make it red white and blue. Great!

DAVIE: Ye'll have tae give it a name.

BILLY: How about *No Surrender?*

DAVIE: Sometimes they're called after the places they're built. *City of Glasgow.*

ALEC: Ah thought ae a name. *Star of the Sea.*

DAVIE: That's nice.

BILLY: Did ye make it up?

ALEC: Ah read it in a book.

BILLY: Oh aye. Its no bad right enough. But ah still prefer *No Surrender.*

DAVIE: Aye, you would!

(ALEC *makes boat sail*)

BILLY: Eh . . . (*To* DAVIE) ah had a word wi that bookie, about the wee . . . business.

DAVIE: What did he say?

BILLY: Och, he tried tae come the hard man. But ah don't think he'll bother ye again.

DAVIE: Thanks.

BILLY: See ye. (*To* ALEC) Cheerio wee yin.

ALEC: Cheerio. An thanks.

BILLY: Nae bother.

(*Exit*)

ALEC: (*To* DAVIE) When ye gonnae fix it?

DAVIE: (*Cheerful*) Soon. Just you wait an see!

(*Dark. Light on* DAVIE, *forward*)

DAVIE: It was wan a thae dark closes. Nae lights workin. Stink fae the back close – drains an cats an God knows what. That's where they were waitin. Heard a noise an they were comin at me. Two ae them. In wi the heid, the boot. Slammed me against the wa. Butt in the face. They grabbed ma briefcase. Ah swung wi the torch, got one ae them. Ya Bastard. Brained him. Then they got me down. Kicked me in the ribs. Got off their marks an left me. Took ma briefcase. Tick money. The lot. Everything except ma torch.

(*Lights come up a little,* ALEC *takes torch*)

ALEC: It's got a dent in it.

DAVIE: Guy must have had a thick skull!

(ALEC *wields torch like club*)

Ah've seen the day when ah could've stiffened the pair ae them. Used tae be pretty useful. Flyweight. Ah knew Benny Lynch ye know. Tapped me for ten bob the week before he died.

(ALEC *is shining torch round about*)

Don't waste the batteries son.

(ALEC *switches off torch. Cut lights. Dark*)

(ALEC, DAVIE, BILLY, IAN, *home from the football match*)

BILLY: (*Sings*)

Sure it's old but it is beautiful

And its colours they are fine . . .

DAVIE: Christsake Billy, ye'll get us hung!

BILLY: It's a protestant country isn't it? An ah'm not ashamed tae show ma colours. (*more conversational tone*) Wasnae a bad game aw the same.

DAVIE: Well, it wasnae exactly the greatest Rangers team ah've seen.

BILLY: Now Willie Thornton, there was a centre forward. Wan game, they were playin Celtic at Ibrox. Nothin each, a minute tae go. Waddell gets it tae the byeline an slings it across, and there's Thornton comin in like a bullet. An'm no kiddin ye, he just dived full-length, met the baw aboot *that* height aff the grun. Just rocketed aff his heid an intae the net. Keeper never got a sniff at it. An there wis Thornton, face doon in the mud – must've been embedded in it, aboot six inches deep. They had tae prise him oot!

That was some team they had then. Wee Tony Gillick at inside right. Waddell on the wing. An the defence! Big George Young, Sammy Cox, Tiger Shaw, big Woodburn before he got suspended. There were like . . . iron.

DAVIE: 'They shall not pass!'

BILLY: An if the other team *did* get through, there was Jerry Dawson tae stop them. What a keeper!

DAVIE: Ah remember wance, he was aff his line, an the forward comin in just lobbed him – cheeky as ye like – just flicked it over his heid. It was goin, aw the way . . . Christ, does Jerry no fling himself *backwards* – ah'm no kiddin ye, right back like that, parallel tae the grun, and he clutched it, about an inch fae the line. Talk about acrobatic! Never seen anythin like it!

IAN: Did ye ever see Alan Morton?

DAVIE: The wee blue devil! Oh aye, ah saw him when ah was wee. He was one ae the Wembley Wizards. A real ballplayer, ye know what ah mean? Pure skill. An it wasnae so easy then – the baw was heavier an they aw wore these big clumpetty boots up tae here. But ye should've seen the wee man dribblin. Incredible! An wan time he scored direct fae a corner kick. Curved it right in. Magic!

ALEC: Charlie Tully did that.

DAVIE: Don't talk tae me about Tully! Morton was in a different class. He was a real gentleman tae. Never committed a deliberate foul in his life.

BILLY: A protestant!

*(They laugh. Boys take imaginary ball and run across stage.
DAVIE and BILLY go out)*

ALEC: C'mon, ah'll be Alan Morton, you be Willie Thornton.

IAN: But they didnae play at the same time.

ALEC: Disnae matter. We can kid on. Use yer imagination.

IAN: Awright, it's the greatest Rangers team of all time, gathered
together for one special game.

ALEC: The Championship of the Universe!

IAN: Playin on the moon.

ALEC: Against Martian Celtic! Biggest buncha zombies ye ever
saw!

IAN: Everybody's weightless. Morton crosses an Thornton jumps
50 feet in the air.

ALEC: He misses and the baw goes into orbit.

IAN: So they bring on a new baw. Weighs half a ton.

ALEC: They're aw wearin lead boots. There's been some terrible
tackles.

IAN: The Martian goalie's got eight arms and six legs.

ALEC: The centre-forward's got four heids.

IAN: Typical fenians!

ALEC: We're intae injury time. Morton's got the ball. *(Dribbles)* He
beats one tackle, beats two, passes it to Thornton. *(Passes)*

IAN: Back to Morton. *(Passes)*

ALEC: To Thornton. *(Passes)*

IAN: To Morton. *(Passes)*

ALEC: The goalie comes rushin out. He's about ten feet four.
Morton slips it through his three pairs of legs, gives it back
to Thornton. *(Passes)*

IAN: *(Shoots)* An it's a goal!

ALEC: An there goes the final whistle. It's all over. Rangers are the champions of the whole Universe!

IAN: Ea-sy!

ALEC: See! Ah told ye ye could use yer imagination.

IAN: Imagine *really* bein a fitba player. Gettin *paid* for it! Be better than anythin.

ALEC: Best job in the whole world.

IAN: Better than bein a painter!

ALEC: Or a sailmaker.

IAN: Or a tick man.

(*They exit,* DAVIE *and* BILLY *enter, opposite sides of stage*)

BILLY: What's up wi your face?

(DAVIE *shakes head*)

What's the matter?

DAVIE: Ah just got ma jotters. Week's notice.

BILLY: Jesus Christ! What for?

DAVIE: Ach! They're sayin the book's a dead loss. They're gonnae shut it awthegether. Put the sherriff's officers on tae the folk that still owe money.

BILLY: Bastards.

DAVIE: Gettin that doin just finished it. Losin the money an the ledgers an everythin.

BILLY: But that wasnae your fault!

DAVIE: Try tellin *them* that! So that's me. Scrubbed. Again. Laid off. Redundant. Services no longer required. Just like that. Ah don't know. Work aw yer days an what've ye got tae show for it? Turn roon an kick ye in the teeth. Ah mean, what *have* ye got when ye come right down tae it. Nothin.

BILLY: Ah might be able tae get ye a start in our place. Cannae promise mind ye. An if there was anythin it wouldnae be much. Maybe doin yer sweeper up or that.

DAVIE: Anythin's better than nothin.

BILLY: An once yer in the place, ye never know. Somethin better might come up.

DAVIE: (*Dead*) Aye.

BILLY: Likes ae a storeman's job or that.

DAVIE: Aye.

BILLY: We never died a winter yet, eh?

(DAVIE *nods.* BILLY *exits*)

DAVIE: Scrubbed. Get yer jacket on. Pick up yer cards. On yer way pal! Out the door.

(ALEC *is playing with yacht, positions fid like bowsprit, bow like mast, tries to make 'sail' with cellophane, can't hold all the separate bits, drops them.* DAVIE *comes in behind him*)

Bit of bad news son.

(*Pause*)

Ah've lost ma job. They gave me ma books.

ALEC: What'll we dae?

DAVIE: Billy says he might be able tae fix me up wi somethin. Wouldnae be much. (*Shrugs*) Better than nothin. Ach, that was a lousy job anyway. Ah'm better off out ae it. Whatever happens.

Place is a right mess eh. Amazin how it gets on top of ye.

ALEC: Ah'll shove this in the Glory Hole. Out the road.

(*Folds up cellophane, puts tools in bag and picks up bow, yacht, carries the lot and exits*)

DAVIE: Ach aye. Not to worry. Never died a winter yet.

(*Fade lights. Two notes on mouth organ, fade*)

ACT TWO

(DAVIE is sitting in chair, reading newspaper. ALEC enters, singing.)

ALEC: *(Sings)*

> Give me oil in my lamp keep me burning
>
> Give me oil in my lamp I pray
>
> Halleluja!
>
> Give me oil in my lamp keep me burning
>
> Keep me burning till the break of day

DAVIE: Right wee religious fanatic these days eh? What is it the night then, the bandy hope?

ALEC: Christian Endeavour. Band a Hope's on Thursday.

DAVIE: Ah thought Christian Endeavour was last night?

ALEC: That was just the Juniors. Tonight's the real one.

DAVIE: Are ye no too young?

ALEC: The minister says ah can come.

DAVIE: Is that because ye were top in the bible exam?

ALEC: Top equal. Ah don't know if that's why. He just said ah could come.

DAVIE: Ach well, keeps ye aff the streets!

ALEC: Ah'll be the youngest there.

DAVIE: Mind yer heid in the door. Ye'll get stuck!

ALEC: *(Peering at himself in shaving mirror)* This wee mirror ae yours is really stupid!

DAVIE: What's up wi it?

ALEC: Look at it! There's a big crack doon the middle. The two halfs don't sit right – aw squinty.

DAVIE: Does me fine for shavin.

ALEC: Canny get a good look at yerself. It's dead annoyin.

DAVIE: Ach away ye go!

ALEC: Seen ma bible?

DAVIE: Try lookin where ye left it. (ALEC *looks around*) What's that under thae papers?

ALEC: Where?

DAVIE: There. (*Picks up book*) Naw. It's yer prize fae the Sunday School. (*Reads*) The Life of David Livingstone. Good book that. Ah read it when ah was a boy, when ah was in the Boy's Brigade. Funny, it made me want to be a missionary maself. Great White Doctor an that. Off tae darkest Africa.

ALEC: So what happened?

DAVIE: Och, ye know. Just . . . drifted away fae it. Ended up in darkest Govan instead! (*reads label in book*) Glasgow City Mission. First Prize (Equal). Bible knowledge.

ALEC: The questions were a skoosh. Who carried Christ's cross on the way to Calvary? And stuff fae the Catechism. Into what estate did the fall bring mankind? Dead easy. Just a matter of rememberin.

DAVIE: Ach aye, ye take yer brains fae yer mother son. She was clever ye know. Just wurnae the same opportunities when we were young. You stick in son. Get yerself a good education. Get a decent job. Collar and tie. Never have tae take yer jacket off.

(*Reads*) First Prize.

Ah was in the B.B. for a long time ye know.

Sure and Stedfast! (*Sings*)

Will your anchor hold

In the storms of life

When the clouds unfold

Their wings of strife

ALEC: Ah've still got yer badge for long service.

DAVIE: Ah was a sergeant.

ALEC: Ah've got quite a lot of badges now. There's that Rangers supporter's badge Uncle Billy gave me, wi the lion rampant on it. And the army badge that's shaped like a flame.

DAVIE: Engineers.

ALEC: Christian Endeavour's got a badge. It's a dark blue circle wi a gold rim, and CE in gold letters. Maybe ah'll get one the night. Some ae the teachers have got another badge. It's green wi a gold lamp – a sorta oil lamp, like Aladdin's.

DAVIE: Is there gonnae be any other youngsters there the night?

ALEC: Just Norman. (*Distaste in his voice*)

DAVIE: The Minister's boy. Ye don't like him do ye?

ALEC: He's a big snotter. Thinks he's great.

DAVIE: Was he top in the bible exam as well?

ALEC: Top equal. (DAVIE laughs)

DAVIE: That Minister's a nice wee fella. That time he came up here, after yer mother died, we had quite a wee chat.

ALEC: Aye ye told me.

DAVIE: Ah think he got a surprise. Wi me no goin to church an that, he must've thought ah was a bit ae a heathen. Expected to find me aw bitter, crackin up, y'know?

ALEC: Aye ah know.

DAVIE: But ah wisnae. Ah showed him ma long-service badge fae the B.B. Even quoted scripture at him.

ALEC: Aye.

DAVIE: In my father's house there are many mansions, ah said. That's the text they read at the funeral!

ALEC: Time ah was goin.

DAVIE: He wanted me tae come tae church, but ah cannae be bothered wi aw that. Anyway, you're goin enough for the two ae us these days, eh?

ALEC: Aye. Here's ma bible. (*Picks it up from under newspapers*) Well. Cheerio da.

DAVIE: See ye after son.

(ALEC *crosses stage, whistling 'Give Me Oil in My Lamp'. Football rolls across.* IAN *enters*)

IAN: That baw! (ALEC *passes ball to him*) Comin doon for a game?

ALEC: Naw.

IAN: How no?

ALEC: Ah'm goin somewhere.

IAN: The Mission?

ALEC: Aye.

IAN: Again? Ye never come oot wi us these days.

ALEC: There's a lot ae things on at the Mission.

IAN: Ye don't have tae go tae them aw!

ALEC: Ah like it.

IAN: Aw well. Suit yerself. (*Dribbles ball round* ALEC)

(*Chanting*)

Will ye come to the mission

Will ye come, will ye come

Will ye come to the mission

Will ye come . . . (*Laughs*)

Well! (*Calls out as he exits*)

Gawn yersel!

Ah'll get ye!

Ah'll let ye!

ALEC: Ian thought I was soft in the head for going so much to the Mission. He couldn't understand. I felt this glow. It was good to feel good. It had come on stronger since my mother had died.

Ah cut across the back courts. Ah could hear Ian and his mates shoutin and laughin in the distance, makin a rammy. Somebody kicked over a midden bin, smashed a bottle. Some auld wifie shouted at them and they scattered. I got ma head down, hurried through a close and out into the street.

When ah got to the Mission ah was early. There was only a handful of people, sittin talkin at the front. Nobody even noticed me comin in.

Norman was busy stackin hymnbooks. He saw me and went out into the back room. Then the minister waved me over. He introduced me to this middle-aged African couple.

These are our very special guests, he says. Mr and Mrs Lutula. From Africa.

How do you do, we all say, an everybody shakes hands. Then there's this awkward silence. An ah'm standin there like a stookie, no knowin where tae look. Then the conversation sorta picks up again, round about me. But ah can feel the big black woman lookin at me. Tell me, she says – big deep voice like a man's – When did the Lord Jesus come into *your* heart? Pardon? I says. Terrified! She looks right *at* me. Ah said, when did the Lord Jesus come into your heart, child?

That was what I thought she'd said.

And she wanted an answer. From me!

I looked down at the floor.

I could feel myself blush,

What kind of question was that to ask?

How was I supposed to answer it?

Why didn't she ask me something straightforward?

Who carried Christ's cross on the way to Calvary?

Simon of Cyrene.

Into what estate did the fall bring mankind?

The fall brought mankind into an estate of sin and misery.

(*Tugs at collar*)

It's hot in here. Feelin a wee bit sick.

Ah'll just go outside for a minute, get some fresh air . . .

Ah'm trippin over ma own feet.

Knock over a pile of hymnbooks. Jesus Christ!

Out into the street, walkin faster, runnin, away fae the Mission, through a close, into the back court . . .

The night air was cool. I stopped an leaned against a midden wall. When did the Lord Jesus come into my heart? I could have said it was when my mother died. That would have sounded pious.

But I didn't think it was true. I didn't know. That was it, I didn't know.

If the Lord Jesus had come into my heart, I should know.

The back court was quiet. Just the sound of the TV from this house or that.

Dark tenement blocks.

I kicked over a midden bin, and ran.

Nearer home, I slowed down again.

My father would ask why ah was back so early.

(*Throws down book*)

DAVIE: What's the matter?

ALEC: Nothin.

DAVIE: What d'ye mean nothin?

ALEC: Nothin Nothin Nothin!

DAVIE: Yer face is trippin ye. C'mon. Cheer up. It might never happen!

ALEC: Don't annoy me!

DAVIE: Oh ho! Fightin talk!

(*Squares up to him, sparring, flicks a few imaginary punches*) C'mon! You an me doon the back wi the jackets aff. Three rounds.

ALEC: (*Sparring, taking him up*) Yes and here we go. Three rounds to decide the flyweight championship of this hoose. Me in the blue corner, the challenger, up-and-coming. The auld man in the red corner . . .

DAVIE: Never mind the auld . . .

ALEC: The auld man . . . the defending champion . . . once beat a man that knew a wumman that maulacated Benny Lynch's granny . . .

DAVIE: (*Drops guard, offended*) Ah knew Benny Lynch! Me an Benny were like that. (*Crosses fingers*)

ALEC: Aye ah know. Ye lent him a fiver ten minutes before he died. (*Swings a punch*)

DAVIE: (*Guard up again*) It was ten bob and it was a week! Terrible state he was in.

ALEC: Probably used the ten bob tae buy his last bottle of plonk. The one that laid him out for the count. (*Pokes* DAVIE *in stomach*)

DAVIE: Ya wee bugger!

(*Rains a flurry of blows, just short of* ALEC's *face*)

ALEC: (*Giving up*) Awright! Awright! (DAVIE *stops*) You should teach me how tae box.

Ah could join a club.

DAVIE: Ach naw son. Boxin's a mug's game. Ye don't want tae waste yer time. Ah didnae stick it.

Chucked it when ah met yer mother.

Can do yerself serious damage. Ah was lucky.

Only got a broken nose.

ALEC: D'ye know that joke?

Hey, you wi the broken nose, sing Clementine.

Ah havnae got a broken nose an a canny sing.

Wallop!

(*Holds nose, sings*) Oh ma darlin, Oh ma darlin . . .

DAVIE: (*Laughs*) Definitely a mug's game.

ALEC: Ah was thinkin more just for self-defence an that.

DAVIE: Aye, well. Could show ye the basics ah suppose.

Nae harm in knowin how tae look after yerself.

Specially in a place like this.

Course the likes ae Benny Lynch an these blokes it was the only way tae get out. Fightin. (*Looks at* ALEC) You'll get out usin yer brains but.

ALEC: This exam's comin up.

DAVIE: You'll do it. Make a big difference. Goin tae a good school. Go on tae the University. Decent job.

ALEC: Never have tae take ma jacket off!

(*Puts on jacket, tie, takes pen from inside pocket, sits down at table*)

"By selling a piano for £32 a dealer lost one ninth of the cost price. What would he have gained it he had sold it for £38?"

Christ that's hard. Ah'll come back to it.

"Two pipes fill a bath in 7½ minutes and 10 minutes respectively, while a third pipe can empty it in 15 minutes. If the three pipes are opened together, in what time will the bath be half full?"

Ah'll try the next one.

"A contractor engaged to do a piece of work in 36 days and employed 52 men. After 20 days the work was only half done. How many additional men must he employ to finish the work in the given time?"

God Almighty. Ah cannae do any of these!

Just calm down. Take it easy. There's a knack to it. That's all. Just a matter of seein through it. Take them one at a time. Now.

By selling a piano for £32.

God.

Two pipes fill a bath.

Be nice to have a house wi a bath.

36 days 52 men.

Maybe if ah do wee diagrams. *Picture it.*

Selling a piano.

Do a wee drawin of Fats Domino tinklin the ivories.

Hey, you wid the broken nose, sing Red Sails in the Sunset. Ah ain't got no broken nose an ah can't sing. Wallop!

In what time will the bath be half full?

Did ye ever hear anythin so daft? Who's gonnae run water intae a bath an out again at the same time?

Stupid.

Just as stupid as me sittin here tryin to work it all out. Bet Ian's out playin football right now. Lucky dog.

52 men 36 days finish the work in the given time.

52 men. One for every week in the year. They're diggin a hole or somethin. Navvies. Takin their jackets off.

36 days hath September. That's no right.

52 men are selling a bath. How long will it take them to play the piano?

(*Holds nose, sings*)

Red sails in the sunset

Way out on the sea . . .

Wallop!

(*Stands up, takes off tie, shoves it in pocket, scrumples up question-paper*)

IAN: (*Entering*) How was the exam?

ALEC: Terrible. Boggin.

IAN: D'ye think ye failed?

ALEC: Aye. English was easy. Arithmetic was murder.

IAN: Ach well. Be a buncha snobs at that school anyway. Aw toffeenosed wee shites.

ALEC: Yer probably right. They havenae even got a fitba team. Play rugby.

IAN: Tellt ye. Snobs.

(ALEC *kicks scrumpled paper up in the air, takes ball from* IAN'*s feet and kicks it offstage*)

ALEC: Blooter!

(IAN *chases ball.* DAVIE *enters with envelope*)

DAVIE: It's the results.

ALEC: You open it.

DAVIE: (*Opens, reads*) You've passed!

ALEC: (*Grabs letter, reads*) "We have pleasure in informing you . . ." Ah've passed! (*Jumps in the air like a footballer*) Wo ho! Ya beauty!

DAVIE: Ah knew ye could do it!

ALEC: Must have got a good mark in the English.

DAVIE: Nae bother.

ALEC: Ah'll go an dae a lap of honour roon the street, eh? (*Punches arms in air*) Ea-sy! Ea-sy!

DAVIE: Yer teacher'll be pleased.

ALEC: (*Reads*) "You have been awarded a bursary . . ."

It's great. Means ye get aw yer books an fees an everythin. Ah'll need tae get a school uniform. Blazer an tie an aw that.

DAVIE: That's right. Need tae get ye kitted out.

ALEC: How ye gonnae get the money?

DAVIE: Don't you worry about that. Ah'll think ae somethin.

ALEC: (*Runs, punching the air*) Hullaw! (IAN *enters*) Ah passed ma exam!

IAN: Ah thought ye'd failed?

ALEC: So did ah!

IAN: Aw well, that's it then.

ALEC: Ah couldnae believe it.

IAN: Right wee brainbox, eh! (*Laughs*)

ALEC: What's funny?

IAN: Ah can just see you wi the wee uniform. The wee cap an that!

ALEC: Aye. Well. It's a good school.

IAN: Ye'll need tae build yerself up, for playing rugby!

ALEC: Ye have tae be about 6 feet square an weigh 20 stone.

IAN: There's always cricket! (*Mimics bowler, exaggerated mincing run*) Howzat! (*Laughs*) It's aw boys at that school, intit?

ALEC: Aye.

IAN: Nae lassies?

ALEC: Naw.

IAN: Don't fancy that. Hey, ah'd watch ma bum if ah was you! Suppose ye'll be stayin on, sittin Highers an aw that?

ALEC: Hope so.

IAN: Ah couldnae stick it. Imagine still bein at school when yer eighteen or that. Soon as ah'm auld enough ah'm chuckin it. Gettin maself a job.

ALEC: Ye still gonnae try an get in wi yer da?

IAN: Probably. Thing is but, we might be movin away.

ALEC: Where?

IAN: Don't know yet. If ma da gets made redundant he says he'll have tae go where the work is. Could be anywhere. Even England. Corby or that.

ALEC: Too bad.

IAN: Anyway, ah'll be seein ye.

ALEC: Aye. Cheerio.

IAN: An remember, watch yer bum! (*Shouts back as he exits*) Howzat!

(DAVIE *enters holding blazer,* ALEC *puts it on*)

ALEC: It's a wee bit big.

DAVIE: Ye'll grow intae it. Means ye'll no need a new one next year.

ALEC: How did ye manage tae get it?

DAVIE: Got it on tick. Pay it up. Nae bother. (*Pats ALEC's shoulders*) Aw son. Ah wish yer mother could see ye.

ALEC: Ah know.

DAVIE: This is a great chance yer gettin son. Great opportunity. Get yerself a good education. Nothin tae beat it.

ALEC: (*Coming forward*) First conjugation.

Amos, amas, amat, amamus, amatis, amant.

I love, you love, he she or it loves,

We love, you love, they love.

Half the class got belted for not bein able to do that.

Amare.

To love.

Wallop.

Same in music, for the ones that couldn't sightread.

Every Good Boy Deserves Favour.

Or in physics and chemistry if you messed up an experiment. $C + O_2$ gives CO_2.

Matter can neither be created nor destroyed.

Glasgow made the Clyde, the Clyde made Glasgow.

Amazin the things ye remember.

Algebra Geometry Trigonometry.

What is the square root of minus one?

Religious Education, one period a week.

The Apostle's Creed.

I believe for every drop of rain that falls, a flower grows.

Elementary calculus.

The approach to Standard English.

Earth hath not anything to show more fair.

Tomorrow and tomorrow and tomorrow.

Future.

Amabo.

I will love.

Electricity. Magnetic flux.

The periodic table of the elements.

Analyse. Parse. Conjugate. Decline.

Prove. Discuss. Explain. With diagrams.

Future Perfect. Nothing to beat it.

A good education.

Tomorrow and tomorrow.

First year, second year, third year bursary.

Fourth year 'O' grade, fifth year Highers.

University here I come.

(*Pause*)

Ready or not. (*Runs off*)

DAVIE: Factory's shuttin doon right enough son. Billy's no so bad, he'll get redundancy money. Ah havnae been there long enough. Still. Not to worry, eh!

ALEC: (*Comes back with record player*) And what does your father do? He's not actually working just now, but he's a sailmaker to trade. Sounds fascinating. Aye.

This has just been lyin in the Glory Hole.

DAVIE: What did ye drag it out for?

ALEC: A boy in ma class lent me some records.

DAVIE: Used tae have a lot of records. Tchaikovsky. John McCormack. Fats Waller.

ALEC: What happened to them?

DAVIE: Had tae sell them. Coupla quid for the lot.

(ALEC *lifts lid of record player, checks playing arm, dusts it etc . . .*)

Any idea what ye'd like for yer tea?

ALEC: (*Preoccupied*) Ah'm no bothered.

DAVIE: Maybe yer no bothered, but how about makin a suggestion once in a while!

ALEC: What's the matter?

DAVIE: D'ye think it's easy? Day after day after day, havin tae think ae somethin. An once in a blue moon ah ask for a wee suggestion and what dae ah get?

(*Mimics boy*) Ah'm no bothered

Disnae matter

It's aw wan tae me.

ALEC: Aye, but if you're askin me it means *you're* stuck. You cannae think ae anythin an ah'm supposed tae come up wi somethin brilliant. Out the blue. It's no as if we've got a lot of choice. Sausages, mince, fish . . .

DAVIE: How about stew?

ALEC: Well . . .

DAVIE: See, there yar! Ye say yer no bothered but ye don't fancy stew!

ALEC: If ye make stew ah'll eat it. It's just . . .

DAVIE: What?

ALEC: Well, there's more tae stew than just shovin a dod a meat in the pot wi an oxo cube and slappin it on the plate wi a slice a bread.

DAVIE: Oh ah'm helluva sorry. Ah didn't realise we had a gourmet in the family!

ALEC: Ah think ah'll become a vegetarian. Ah was readin this book . . .

DAVIE: Christ is that the next thing?

ALEC: What d'ye mean?

DAVIE: The next craze. We've been through the dinky toys and the fitba an the pop stars. Is it gonnae be long hair an ban the bomb noo?

ALEC: Och forget it! (DAVIE *goes out*)

Forget everythin.

Wish ye could.

There's somethin ah *have* forgotten.

Somethin ah've lost.

What is it?

God knows.

(*He rushes across, takes record from briefcase and puts it on turntable.*

Tape 'My Generation', The Who. ALEC *jumps around to the music, jabbing, kicking, aggressive.*

Music stops dead, lights go dim)

ALEC: What's up? How come there's nae light?

DAVIE: (*Re-entering*) Electricity got cut off son. Couldnae pay the bill.

ALEC: Aw Christ.

DAVIE: It's awright. Ah'll borrow the money. Get it put back on.

ALEC: Ma bursary money'll be comin through this week, can pay it wi that.

DAVIE: Right! That's great!

ALEC: Ah wanted tae buy some things wi it. A shirt an that.

DAVIE: Might still be enough.

ALEC: They charge ye extra for reconnection.

DAVIE: Don't worry. We'll work it out. C'mon! You tell me what kinda shirt ye want an ah'll get it when ah'm in payin the bill. Right?

(ALEC *nods*)

Nae bother. Hey there's a coupla pies in the oven.
Candlelight dinner for two sir?

(ALEC *smiles in spite of himself. They exit*)

(BILLY *enters, wearing overalls carrying paint pots, brushes
etc. Small canvas bag over shoulder containing sandwiches,
flask of tea etc. He is cleaning paint from his hands*)

BILLY: (*Calling off*) Hey Michaelangelo! Ye finished that ceiling?

IAN: (*Off*) Aye.

BILLY: Ah'm oot here when yer ready.

IAN: (*Entering, also in overalls, cleaning hands*) What's for wur
piece?

BILLY: Don't know. Cheese or spam or somethin.

IAN: (*Looks in bag, opens sandwich*) Cheese. (*Opens second
sandwich*) Spam.

BILLY: Ah'm easy. (IAN *passes him sandwich. They eat*) Piece
perfect piece!

IAN: Piecework! (*They laugh*) Feels funny workin on a Saturday.

BILLY: Aye. Ah'm sorry yer missin the match. But just think ae
the money yer rakin in wi aw this overtime. Two nights an
a Saturday an Sunday.

IAN: (*Noncommittal*) Aye.

BILLY: An it's no as if it's gonnae be every week. They're just in
a hurry tae get this place open on time.

IAN: What kinda shop's it gonnae be?

BILLY: Licensed Grocer's ah think.

Be nice that, havin yer ain business.

Ye know, just after the war, when ah got ma demob
money, ah was gonnae go in wi yer Uncle Davie.

IAN: Daein what?

BILLY: He had this idea tae raise poultry! He'd read a coupla
books. Eggs were still on ration ye see. He reckoned we'd
make a fortune. Fresh farm eggs!

IAN: So how d'ye no dae it?

BILLY: Och. Ah thought it was takin too much ae a chance.

IAN: Ah like Uncle Davie.

BILLY: Aw aye. His heid's in the clouds mind ye!

IAN: Ah got a letter fae Alec. He's still at school. Can ye imagine!

BILLY: Be worth it when he's finished.

Ach aye. Be awright bein yer ain boss right enough. Naebody tellin ye what tae dae. A wee paint shop would dae fine eh? Need tae make sure it was gonnae work but. Line up a coupla nice wee contracts. Like paintin the Forth Bridge!

IAN: That goes on forever.

BILLY: That's right. Just get tae the end an it's time tae start aw over again.

IAN: Imagine bein stuck up there on wan a thae big girders. The wind blowin aboot ye!

BILLY: Bad enough when ah worked in the yards. Daein a boat in the dry dock. Slung over the side in wan a thae wee cradles. Fifty feet aff the grun!

Thing is tae, ah've never had much ae a head for heights.

IAN: How did ye manage?

BILLY: Just had tae. Nothin else for it. Keep yer eyes on the wee bit yer workin on an don't look doon!

IAN: Makes yer hands go aw sweaty just thinkin about it!

BILLY: Ach, ye get used tae it. Same as anythin else.

We'll have ye up there spraypaintin a big gas tank. Or wan a thae oilrigs.

IAN: Ah could spray ma name on it. Ian Rules! OK!

BILLY: Catch ye at that lark an ye'll get a thick ear.

IAN: Och da!

BILLY: Just tellin ye.

IAN: See when you were in the army, did ye like it?

BILLY: It was awright. Ah was lucky mind ye. Didnae see a lot of action. No like some poor buggers. How, ye thinkin about joinin up?

IAN: Ah was readin an advert in the paper. (*Stands with imaginary machinegun*) Join the Professionals.

BILLY: Shows ye a guy playing fitba? Jumpin aff a tank? Sunbathin?

IAN: Aye.

BILLY: They don't show ye the hauf ae it. You'd likely get sent tae Belfast.

IAN: Fight the I.R.A. Be like the Battle ae the Boyne aw over again!

BILLY: It's no just playin at cowboys ye know. These bastards arenae kiddin. Sunbathin by Christ!

IAN: The Navy might be better. See a bit ae the world.

BILLY: See the sea!

Don't get me wrong. Ah've got nothin against it. Queen an Country an aw that. It's just that . . .

IAN: Ah've never even been tae London.

BILLY: Yer no missin much!

IAN: But you can only say that cause ye've been.

BILLY: Look, aw ah'm sayin is don't rush intae anythin, awright? Wance ye sign up that's it. For three year or five year or whatever. Canny say ye don't like it an come runnin hame!

IAN: Ah know that! Anyway ah never *said* ah was gonnae join up. Just said ah was *thinkin* about it.

BILLY: Aye.

We should be thinkin about finishin this job, eh?

Ye fit?

IAN: Aye.

(*They gather up their things*)

BILLY: Green an gold he wants. (*Shakes head*) What can ye dae!

(They exit)

(*Enter* ALEC. *He sits at table, reading*)

DAVIE: (*Off, singing*)

Where the blue of the night

Meets the gold of the day

Someone waits for me.

(DAVIE *enters, drunk*)

DAVIE: Hey, yer auld da knocked it off at the bookies. Nae bother! Went in for a wee half tae celebrate. Then ah met Kenny. Don't know if ye remember him – bloke ah used tae work wi in the yards.

Anyway, that was it. Coupla rounds, wee blether – ye know how it is.

Christ is that the time?

Not to worry. Last orders please. Time gents!

Never mind.

Was a good night. Good Company. Know what ah mean?

Nae harm in it. Coupla halfs. Nice.

(*Noticing* ALEC) Yawright son?

ALEC: (*Not looking up*) Aye.

DAVIE: Ach aye. Yirra good boy. What ye readin?

ALEC: A book.

DAVIE: Naw! *Whit* book!

ALEC: David Copperfield. Got an exam next week.

DAVIE: Dickens, eh? Now yer talkin. Ah've read aw his books. The lot. Got them all out the library. Used tae read a lot ye know. Dickens is the greatest. David Copperfield is it?

ALEC: That's what ah said.

DAVIE: Mr Micawber. Somethin'll turn up, eh?

Income twenty pounds, expenditure nineteen pounds nineteen and six: result happiness.

Income twenty pounds, expenditure twenty pounds and sixpence: result . . .

(*Shrugs*)

Not to worry.

Hey, ah got ye crisps. Bottle ae Irn Bru. (*Puts them on table*)

ALEC: (*Grudging*) Thanks.

DAVIE: Any chance ae a cuppa tea?

ALEC: There's some left in the pot. (DAVIE *pours dregs*)

DAVIE: (*Sings*)

Where the blue of the night

Meets the gold of the day

(*To* ALEC) Cheer up. (*No response*) C'mon. (*Spars*)

ALEC: Chuck it will ye!

DAVIE: Torn face.

ALEC: Ah didnae know where ye wur.

DAVIE: Och . . .

ALEC: Might have been under a bus or anythin.

DAVIE: (*Sighs*) Look. Ah'm sorry, awright? Just . . . wan a these things, ye know.

ALEC: Aye ah know.

DAVIE: Good company. Nae harm in it. Didnae even have a lot tae drink. It's just good tae relax.

Wee refreshment. Ach aye. The patter was good tae.

Kenny's a great Burns man. Could recite Tam O'Shanter tae ye just like that! Yer sittin talkin away and he'll come out wi a line fae it.

Fast by an ingle, bleezing finely

Wi reamin swats that drank divinely

Great stuff eh? Poetry!

Reamin swats!

Anythin for eatin?

ALEC: Naw.

DAVIE: Nothin?

ALEC: Not a thing.

DAVIE: What about that tin a soup?

ALEC: Ah had it for ma tea.

DAVIE: Oh aye. An the creamed rice?

ALEC: Ah ate that tae.

DAVIE: Themorra ah'll get a nice bit steak. Have it wi chips. Fried tomatoes! Is there no even any bread?

ALEC: Nothin.

DAVIE: Can ah take a couple ae yer crisps?

ALEC: Help yerself.

DAVIE: Just a couple. (*Eats crisps, swigs iron brew from bottle*) Reamin swats!

There was this lassie there. In the company like. Peggy her name was. Friend ae Kenny's. Helluva nice tae talk tae. Know what ah mean? Just a really nice person.

ALEC: Oh aye. (*Bangs down book*)

DAVIE: What's *up* wi you?

ALEC: Oh nothin. Nothin at all. Everythin's just hunky-dory!

(*Wipes bottle, swigs. Looks suspiciously at* DAVIE)

Did you gamble wi that bursary money?

DAVIE: Just a coupla quid.

There was gonnae be nothing left after ah'd paid the light bill. Had tae take a chance.

ALEC: Did ye *pay* the bill?

DAVIE: First thing themorra mornin.

ALEC: Don't suppose ye got ma shirt either?

DAVIE: Themorra. Ye can wear it at the weekend. Look like a real spiv!

Ah hear ye've got a wee girlfriend!

ALEC: Who told you that?

DAVIE: Oh, a wee bird told me! What's the lassie's name?

ALEC: What does it matter?

DAVIE: Can you no talk tae me these days? Can ye no tell me *anythin*? Think ah came fae another planet.

ALEC: One time when ah was really wee ah went tae this birthday party – wee lassie doon the road. Must have been ma first party, and we played aw the wee kissin games, ye know. Postman's knock. Bee Baw Babbity.

Anyway, ah came hame dead excited.

An you said, how was the party?

An ye said, did ye kiss the girls and make them cry?

An ah was that embarrased, ah walloped ye wan.

Slapped ye right in the face.

An then ye got mad at me.

DAVIE: Ah'm no suprised!

ALEC: But ye didnae skelp me or anythin. Ye just shoved me away and told me ah was a bad bad bad boy.

DAVIE: Ah don't even remember it.

ALEC: Bad. Bad. Bad. Made me feel dirty. Been better if ye'd just hit me back. But ye didnae. Ye held a grudge.

DAVIE: Christsake, you're the wan that remembers it.

You're the wan that's holdin the grudge.

Ah mean it was nothin!

ALEC: Aye, tae you! That's what ah mean!

DAVIE: Ah give up!

ALEC: Ye always do.

DAVIE: Now that's no nice. That's a bit below the belt.

ALEC: Look at the state ae us. We're livin like bloody Steptoe an Son! Nae light. Place is like a midden. When did we last gie it a good clean? Needs gutted. Look at it!

DAVIE: It's hard son. It's no easy on yer own.

ALEC: So ye go an get bevvied. Forget it all.

DAVIE: Ye'd think ah came in steamin every night!

Christ ah need a wee break once in a while. Like the night. Nae harm in it. Good company. Wee sing song. Right gents, a wee bit order there. One singer one song. That lassie Peggy's a rare singer. Sang Honky Tonk Angels.

She's the one ah told ye about.

ALEC: (*Sarcastic*) The really nice person.

DAVIE: She wis.

ALEC: Who was that lady I saw you with last night?

That was no lady, that was a really nice person.

DAVIE: Nae harm in it.

ALEC: It's always the same. Every time ye meet a wumman she's a really really really nice person.

Why don't ye just admit that ye fancy her?

(DAVIE *slaps him, exits*)

Ach aye, yirra good boy son. Wallop!

Bad. Bad. Bad.

(Pause)

Wallop.

(*Darkness. Spotlight on* ALEC)

I keep goin back.

What is it I'm tryin to remember?

What is it I'm tryin to say?

There's somethin I've lost. Something I've forgotten.

Sometimes in the middle of the night . . .

What is it I'm looking for?

God knows.

(*Lights up. He crosses over, picks up yacht.* DAVIE *is sitting in chair, staring into empty hearth*)

Remember this?

DAVIE: Eh? (*Looks*) Oh aye. It's freezin.

ALEC: Nae coal left?

DAVIE: Ah'll get some themorra, when the dole money comes.

ALEC: Ye wouldnae believe some of the stuff that's in the Glory Hole.

DAVIE: Is that where ye wur? Terrible draught comin in that door.

ALEC: Hey, d'ye remember that poem ye used to tell me?

DAVIE: Poem?

ALEC: About the yacht. (*Recites*)

Ah had a yacht

Y'ought tae see it

I actually thought you wrote it, ye know – made it up yourself.

DAVIE: Och naw. Ah learned it fae *ma* father. Ah wis just passing it on.

ALEC: Ah had a yacht . . . (*Shivers*) Hey it really is cold. There must be some auld stuff in that Glory Hole we could burn.

DAVIE: That's a great idea.

ALEC: Place needs gutted anyway. Might as well make a start. (*Goes out*)

(DAVIE *scrumples up papers for fire, rolls some up into 'doughnut' shapes.* ALEC *returns with box of stuff*)

Coupla auld books for a start. (*Reads*) The Approach to Standard English. (*Throws it over*) Ma auld hymnbook (*flicks through pages*).

DAVIE: Cannae burn a hymnbook.

ALEC: How no?

DAVIE: It's just no right.

ALEC: (*Throws hymnbook* to DAVIE) Hey! (*Reads from Catechism*) Into what estate did the Fall bring mankind?

DAVIE: What?

ALEC: Catechism. What is man's chief end?

DAVIE: (*Parrot-fashion*) Man's chief end is to glorify God and to enjoy Him forever.

Ah'd forgotten all that! Used to know it all. Amazin how ye forget.

ALEC: But part of ye remembers everythin. What's the furthest back you can remember?

DAVIE: Don't know. Never really thought about it.

Ah remember goin tae school. Must have been five.

ALEC: Ah remember bein a baby, in the pram. Honest tae God.

Ah remember bein aw tucked up, and the pram shooglin along, and the rain patterin on the hood. Nobody ever believes me.

DAVIE: Ah believe ye.

ALEC: Ah was readin that ye can remember right back before ye were born. Right back tae the womb.

DAVIE: Never heard ae that!

ALEC: In fact some folk say ye remember it aw the time, away at the back ae yer mind. Lake part ae ye never really forgets, an ye've always got a sorta yearnin tae get back tae it.

DAVIE: (*Remembering answer to question*) The fall brought mankind into an estate of sin and misery!

ALEC: We got some stuff about other religions in school. Hinduism an Buddhism an that. Ye know, some ae them talk about God bein male *and* female. Father an Mother. An some ae them don't talk about God at all.

DAVIE: (*Uncomfortable*) Ye have tae believe in somethin. Otherwise . . . (*Shrugs*)

ALEC: In one ae the Buddhist books ah read there was a story about a monk that burned a wooden statue ae the Buddha. 'What d'ye dae that for?' they asked him. "It's freezin" he says. (*Laughs*) Ah think the idea was that everythin's holy. Or nothin. (*Chucks catechism across*) There ye go! (DAVIE *puts it to one side, along with hymnbook. ALEC takes sea-shell from box, holds it up, puts it to his ear*)

You can still hear the sea!

Ah used to think it was the *actual* sea ye could hear. Whatever sea the shell came from. As if the shell had a memory of the sea right inside it. Naw. No a memory, that's the wrong word. More like an echo. As if it had been caught inside.

(*Hands shell to* DAVIE, *who self-consciously holds it to his ear, sighs, puts shell down*)

Remember this? (*Holds up torch*)

DAVIE: Aye. (ALEC *breathes on torch, polishes it on his sleeve, clicks button*)

ALEC: Disnae work.

DAVIE: Batteries'll be dead.

ALEC: Pity. Could've used it tae see intae that recess. Hey, look, it's still got a dent in it where ye thumped that guy.

DAVIE: What a job that wis. Terrible. Ah'm better on the broo than daein that, any day. That bookie's done awright for himself. Two shops he's got. Nae back closes for him noo.

ALEC: Mainsail. That was yer name.

DAVIE: That's right. Ye remember!

ALEC: Tryin the pools!

DAVIE: Still tryin. Ye never know.

ALEC: (*Opens torch, shakes it, peers inside*) Batteries are stuck. Aw covered in green mouldy stuff. What makes it go like that?

DAVIE: Don't know. Just time. Just . . . time. What else is there?

ALEC: (*Looking in box again*) Coupla old comics. Superman. Blackhawk. Creepy Worlds. (*Reads*) Mysterious Voyage. Journey into the Unknown. (*Throws them over*) Another coupla books. Now these are *really* auld. Peoples of the World, and How the Other Man Lives.

DAVIE: Think we picked them up at a jumble sale.

ALEC: Listen to this! The British Working Man. (*Reads*) The life of the British industrial worker differs only in detail from that of his world counterpart. His housing conditions were once poor, but have been greatly improved.

DAVIE: (*Looking at him*) Have they?

ALEC: (*Continues*) The variety of British industrial occupations is almost endless. The worker may be a skilled man or a labourer. He is perhaps at his best in skilled individual occupations as, for example, in the many aspects of shipbuilding or engineering. He works without rush, but consistently.

DAVIE: Aw!

ALEC: (*Continues*) Our man has probably his special interests: football is most certainly one of them. He will follow the fortunes of his local team with great enthusiasm – probably in his youth he was an active player himself. His summer interest in cricket will not be so emotional, but is often deep.

DAVIE: Cricket?

ALEC: (*Continues*) By American standards the British worker is not highly paid, but then the cost of living is much lower.

DAVIE: Nice tae know.

ALEC: (*Continues*) He is greatly interested in social questions. Better housing, old age pensions, security of employment – on these he is now seeing practical results. Education, too, is an increasingly important subject, and many men seek for their sons better opportunities than they themselves enjoyed in their youth. (*Turns pages*) Goes on like this for about ten pages. Then it goes on to Tribes of Africa, and The American Way of Life.

DAVIE: Great stuff.

ALEC: (*Passes over book*) See what the other one's about. How the Other Man Lives. (*Reads*) The Other Man's job so frequently appears more attractive than one's own.

DAVIE: Specially if ye havnae got wan!

Don't suppose there's anythin about sailmakers? Or redundant tick-men!

ALEC: (*Reads*) Farmer . . . Coalminer . . . Ah don't believe it! Bookmaker! (*Turns pages, reads*)

Here, this is good . . . In theory an astute bookmaker should be able to make his book so that he cannot lose. This, however is accomplished only if he can induce a sufficient number of punters to back little-fancied and long-priced animals.

DAVIE: Mugs! Like me!

ALEC: (*Continues*) If there is money for only two or three horses, then the cleverest bookmaker cannot level his book.

DAVIE: Makes yer heart bleed for them, doesn't it!

(ALEC *shuts book, throws it over to* DAVIE)

Ach aye!

ALEC: What is it that gets intae ye? Wi the bettin ah mean?

DAVIE: Ah don't know. Just wan a these things.

Ah suppose it's the feelin you've at least got a *chance*.

Is there any wood in there? The paper just flares up then dies.

(ALEC *empties out contents of box, hands box to* DAVIE)

DAVIE: Great. (*Starts breaking up box,* ALEC *goes out, comes back with canvas tool-bag, cane bow. Fires imaginary arrow*) Bring me my bow of burning gold, eh?

(ALEC *breaks bow for fire*)

That's more like it. (*Warms himself*)

That's the stuff.

ALEC: (*Taking tools from canvas bag*) Look at this.

DAVIE: God. Ma auld sailmakin tools. (*Takes wooden marlinspike*) Ah was an apprentice when ah was your age. Hard work it wis tae.

Ah worked on the Queen Mary ye know.

ALEC: Aye.

DAVIE: Worked on destroyers durin the War. Made gun-covers, awnings, tarpaulins.

Made this wee bag!

ALEC: Did ye?

DAVIE: Oh aye. Used tae make leather wallets an things.

Made a shopping bag for yer mother. Made you a swing! Wi a big sorta bucket seat. Used tae hang it in the doorway there.

ALEC: Ah remember!

You could still be makin things. Sellin them.

(DAVIE *nods, shrugs*)

Could ye no go back tae yer trade?

DAVIE: Nae demand. Was different durin the War. They needed us then awright. Reserved occupation it was. Meant ah couldnae sign up. Been goin downhill since then but. Yards shuttin doon. Look at Harland's. Or where it was. Just a big empty space covered wi weeds.

Yer Uncle Billy had the right idea. Took his redundancy money an moved tae Aberdeen. Doin all right.

ALEC: Ian's an Aberdeen supporter now.

DAVIE: Billy'll disown him for that!

ALEC: Did you ever think about movin?

DAVIE: Thought about it. (*Shrugs*) Thing is Billy bein a painter had more chance ae a job. Ah backed a loser right fae the start. Then it got even worse. They started bringin in aw the manmade fibres, usin machines. Got lassies daein hauf the work. Dead loss.

So for God's sake you dae somethin wi *your* life!

At least we'll be gettin out ae this place when they pull it doon. Get rehoused. Fresh start.

ALEC: Ah've been thinkin da. When ah go tae the University ah might get a wee place ae ma own. Wee bedsit or somethin. Over near the Uni.

DAVIE: Oh aye. Will that no be dear?

ALEC: Shouldnae be too bad.

DAVIE: Whatever ye think.

ALEC: Ah'll see what happens.

DAVIE: Aye.

(*Silence between them.* DAVIE *takes up tools*)

These are made fae lignum vitae.

ALEC: That's Latin. Wood of life.

DAVIE: Hardest wood in the world. Should burn nice an slow. (*Puts in fire*) Thae other tools can go in the midden sometime. (*Watches fire*) Is there anythin else?

ALEC: There's this. (*Indicates chair*)

DAVIE: This is part of the furniture we got when we were married. Got it in Galpern's. That's him that was the Lord Provost. Solid stuff it is too.

Nobody takes the care any more.

Nobody's interested in this auld stuff.

(*He is talking himself into being sad*)

Ah remember when we bought it.

Seems a shame tae break it up. Still

It's a shame tae freeze as well, isn't it.

(*Breaks up chair, they watch it burn*)

ALEC: (*Picks up yacht*) That just leaves this.

DAVIE: Yer Uncle Billy painted it.

ALEC: You were always gonnae fix it up for me.

Ah could always imagine it. Like that song. Red sails in the sunset.

DAVIE: Ah always meant to. Just . . .

ALEC: Just never did.

DAVIE: Story a ma life.

ALEC: (*Comes forward with yacht*) When the last bit of furniture had burned down, I wedged the yacht in the grate.

The flames licked round it.

The paint began to blister and bubble.

Then the wood of the hull caught and burned.

And the yacht had a sail of flame.

And it sailed in the fire, like a Viking longboat, out to sea in a blaze with the body of a dead chief.

And the wood burned to embers. And the iron keel clattered onto the hearth. (*Drops yacht*)

May God bless her and all who sail in her!

Star of the Sea. Stella Maris.

Amabo. I will love.

Amazin the things ye remember.

Glasgow made the Clyde, the Clyde made Glasgow.

Matter can neither be created nor destroyed.

Ah had a yacht

Y'ought tae see it.

DAVIE: Put it in the canal.

Ye can all see it.

(Fade lights)

(*Tape: Fats Domino, Red Sails in the Sunset*)

END OF PLAY

Activities

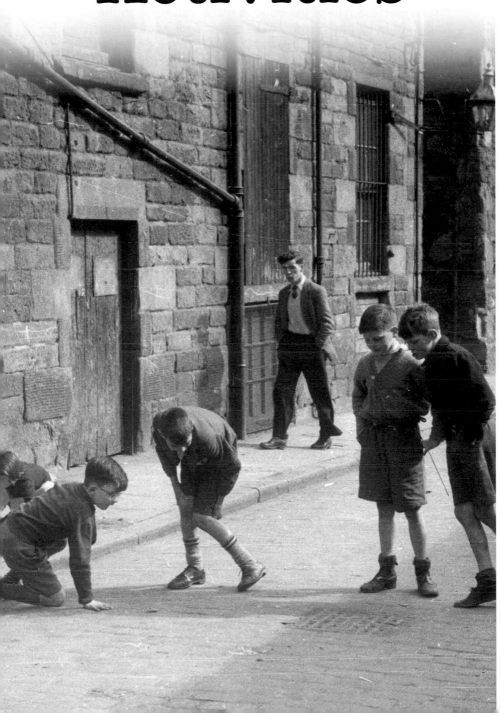

Notes and Questions on the Text

You can use this part of the book to guide you through the play. You'll find notes and pictures to help you understand the text, and questions to help you check what you've learned. Sometimes there will be an instruction box to tell you to pause and do one of the longer tasks from later in the book.

Page	Quotation	Notes
6	'Sometimes I wake up . . .'	Notice that Alec uses standard, formal English to speak to the audience. This is the adult Alec introducing a flashback. When Davie speaks as Alec remembers him, he speaks in Glaswegian Scots.
6	'Ah've got a bit of bad news for ye son.'	**Q1** These words by Davie appear twice on this page. Do you think he really said them twice? If not, why are they in the play twice?
7	'Ah'm no really very hungry.'	This is now the voice of Alec as a child, so he too speaks Glaswegian Scots.
7	'A sign. Jesus to come walking . . .'	This is the first of many references to religion which are important in the play.
7	'blowing on a mouth-organ . . .'	A mouth-organ, or harmonica, is a small, cheap musical instrument, easy to learn.

→

Page	Quotation	Notes
7	'We'd better get this place tidied . . .'	Without the writer saying so, time has moved on and we are now at the day of Alec's mother's funeral.
7	'As long as ye keep movin . . .'	**Q2** Who do you think Davie is talking to in this long speech?
8	'Ah'm shattered.'	**Q3** Davie's words have two possible meanings. What are they?
8	'In the mornin.'	**TASK TIME** Stop here and do the task called Comparing Two Versions which is on page 78 of this book.
8	Lights up	The play only has one formal scene change, but Alan Spence often uses lighting changes or character movements to move on to a slightly different place or time.
8	'Ah had a yacht.'	These two lines are actually a pun, a joke based on the sounds of words. Try saying them in a broad Glasgow accent to see if you can hear how they work.
8	'the Glory Hole'	A built-in cupboard full of stuff that is kept in case it turns out to be useful.

Page	Quotation	Notes
8	'the never never'	Paying for something in small, weekly amounts on hire purchase. It was called this because you never owned something until you'd made the final payment, and you might never get there.
8	'a tick man'	A collector of never never payments who would tick off names in his notebook as he collected each week's money.
8	'that's his trade'	A trade is a skilled manual job, one that takes several years to learn.
9	'Red sails in the sunset'	Music is very important in this play, and this is the first time it is mentioned. **TASK TIME** Look at page 81 where you'll find a list called Music In The Play. This is a good time to start downloading.
10	'when he went tae America.'	Scotland has a long history of emigration as people have left to find jobs and a better way of life abroad. Millions of Americans have Scottish ancestors.
11	'In the middle of the week?'	Davie isn't coping with cooking or running the home, but buying fish suppers is an expense he can't really afford.
12	'Our Lady'	This is a name Catholics would often use for Mary, the mother of Jesus. It's odd that Alec should use this name. He's just mentioned blue grass for Ibrox which suggests he is a Protestant, and further down page 7 he calls Ian stupid for suggesting he might carry a set of rosary beads and cross himself like a Catholic.
12	'the Lifeboys'	A church youth organisation.
13	'ah thought ah saw her.'	**Q4** Why do you think Alec imagined seeing the Virgin Mary? How do you think seeing her made him feel?

Page	Quotation	Notes
14	'Ah hate whelks.'	Whelks are small shellfish, sometimes called sea-snails.
15	'These are called marlinspikes.'	
15	'Make a great chib!'	The word *chib* is a Scots dialect word for a knife. **Q5** What does it say about Ian's character if he sees the marlinspike and immediately imagines using it as a chib?
16	'You've been drinkin. Ah can smell it.'	We've just seen Alec playing with Ian and using his childlike imagination but he suddenly has to cope with his dad's very adult problems.
16	'This is a fid . . . It's a palm'. 	
16	'Maybe ma coupon'll come up this week!'	Davie is talking about the football pools, a form of gambling based on predicting match results. **Q6** What would Davie say if the play was set nowadays?
16	'Two quid!'	This part of the play is set in about 1960. If you spent £2 in 1960 it would buy you as much as you would get for about £39 at 2013 prices. So, Davie has not really had very much success on the football pools.

→

69

Page	Quotation	Notes
16–21		**Q7** What signs can we see on these pages to show that Davie isn't really coping? What other risks is he taking?
20	'a pape'	Slang term for a Catholic.
21	'the broo'	The unemployment benefit office.
21–22		**Q8** What signs do we see on these pages that show Billy is more realistic than his brother Davie? What signs do we see that Billy might be more aggressive than Davie?
22	'Campbeltown tae Glasgow'	Davie and Billy's dad walked 60 miles, which shows how much he wanted the job.
22		**Q9** What does Alec say on this page to show the audience time is passing?
24	'We could go tae America and live wi real Indians.'	What Ian says here turns out to be rather ironic, as by the end of the play he is living in Aberdeen, not America. The person who wrote these notes grew up there and it's not very exciting.
24	'daft wee reservations'	Reservations are areas of land where Native Americans (*'Indians'*) were once encouraged to live. These areas often ended up with many social problems. You might say that the estates people like Alec and Davie were rehoused to in the 1960s were also a bit like reservations and ended up with some of the same problems.
25	'Sweeney Todd'	An eighteenth century London barber who slit his customers' throats before having their body parts baked into pies.
25	'Dickens an that'	If Davie likes Dickens then it seems Alec gets his brains from his dad.

Page	Quotation	Notes
25	'Alan Ladd'	Film star of the 1940s and 50s who often appeared in cowboy films.
26	'orange'	There is a major sectarian Protestant group called the Orange Order.
27	'No Surrender . . . Star of the Sea.'	*No Surrender* is a slogan often used by Protestant Orangemen. None of the characters seem to know that *Star of the Sea* is a name Catholics use for the Virgin Mary.
27		**Q10** Look at the conversation Davie and Billy have about the bookie. What has Billy done?
28		**Q11** Look at Davie's long speech. Was the attack on him planned or random? How do you know?

➜

Page	Quotation	Notes
28	'Benny Lynch'	A Glaswegian who became world lightweight boxing champion but died in 1946 because of alcohol problems. He was aged just 33. **Q12** Why do you think Lynch is such a hero to Davie? In what ways are the two men similar?
28	'its colours they are fine . . .'	Lyrics from the Protestant sectarian song 'The Sash'. These words are also the title of Alan Spence's first book.
30	'Typical fenians!'	This word, used to insult Catholics, seems out of place in this description of the imaginary space football game.
31	'Better than bein a painter. Or a Sailmaker.'	The 1960s, when this play is set, saw the beginning of the celebrity culture we're so used to now.
31	'got ma jotters'	Davie has been fired.
31	'sheriff's officers'	Official debt collectors. They have the legal power to seize people's possessions to cover unpaid debts.
31	'doin yer sweeper up'	This job would be a big come down for Davie who used to work in a skilled trade.
32	'tries to make 'sail' with cellophane'	After all this time has passed, Davie still has not kept his promise to mend the yacht.
32		**Q13** At the end of Act One, Alec shoves the yacht in the Glory Hole. Why is this important? What does it tell us about his relationship with his father?

→

Page	Quotation	Notes
33	'Give me oil in my lamp . . .'	So far the music in the play has been pop, but here Alec is singing a hymn.
33	'Band a Hope'	The Band of Hope was a Christian group aimed at working class children and was strongly anti-alcohol. **Q14** Why do you think Alec is attracted so much to this group?
34		**Q15** What evidence is there on this page to show that when Davie was young he was very like Alec is now?
34	'the Catechism'	A list of questions and answers which people used to learn by heart to help them understand the Christian faith.
35	'another badge'	The badge is the logo of Scripture Union, another Christian youth group.
35	'In my father's house there are many mansions.'	A quotation from the Bible. It means that Heaven has space for lots of different people.
36–39	'Ian thought . . . Ya wee bugger!'	**TASK TIME** Stop here and do the group discussion task on page 83.
40–41	'exam's comin up'	By passing the exam, Alec can go to a private school with more able pupils. Once he's there he can take more exams that will get him into university. Notice how Spence shows us the exam without special scenery or other actors.
42	'bursary'	Money to cover the fees and other costs of going to a certain school.

→

Page	Quotation	Notes
42–43		**Q16** Look at the things Ian says to Alec on these pages. What assumptions does he make about private schools and the people Alec will meet there?
43	'Corby or that.'	Corby, a town in the English midlands, had a huge steelworks. Lots of Scots moved there to work in the 1960s.
43–44		**Q17** Which details on these pages show us that Davie is short of money?
44	'Amos, amas, amat . . .'	Alec is studying Latin and is chanting Latin verbs to memorise them.
44–45	'First conjugation . . . Ready or not.'	Alan Spence makes five years of Alec's life at high school pass in five minutes by just having him remember details of some lessons.
45	'Factory's shuttin doon right enough.'	Just at the point where Alec does so well at school that he can go to university, Davie's life takes another downturn. This is the third job he's lost.
45	'Used tae have a lot of records.'	Davie's choice of music shows how wide and cultured his tastes were. Tchaikovsky was a classical composer, John McCormack an opera singer, and Fats Waller a jazz musician.
46–47		**Q18** Which details on these pages show us Davie is again having trouble coping? **Q19** Which details show us that Alec is growing up to be very different to his father? What do you think has caused these differences?

→

Page	Quotation	Notes
47	'ban the bomb'	In the 1960s many people went on marches organised by the Campaign for Nuclear Disarmament (CND) to protest against Britain having nuclear bombs.
47	'Somethin' ah've lost'	**Q20** What do you think Alec has lost?
47	'My Generation'	The use of this song by The Who tells us the play has reached 1965.

		Q21 Listen to the song or read the lyrics. What is Spence trying to tell us about how Alec feels?
48	'Ye finished that ceiling?'	We can see big differences now between the two cousins, Alec and Ian. Ian has now left education and is working *with* his father while Alec is still at school and often in conflict with Davie.
		Q22 Read pages 48 and 49 again. List all the ways that Davie and Alec are different to Billy and Ian.
48–49		**Q23** What evidence on this page tells us Davie used to have dreams and ambitions?
		Q24 How can we tell that Billy and Ian have made compromises or sacrifices so they can have enough money?
50	'Shows ye a guy playing fitba? . . . thinkin about finishin this job eh?'	**Q25** Read the conversation between Ian and his dad. What does it show about each of them? What does it show us about their relationship?

→

Page	Quotation	Notes
52	'Mr Micawber . . . Not to worry.'	The fact that Davie remembers these words from Dickens shows how clever he is, but the words are also ironic. Mr Micawber is famous for never having enough money and hoping something better will turn up. At the bottom of the page Davie again shows his intelligence by reciting Robert Burns but this time the irony is that he chooses a section about drunkenness.
55	'Steptoe an Son!'	A very popular 1960s TV comedy about a father and son who lived together and ran a scrapyard. The son, Harold, was always trying to improve himself or get away to a better life, but never managed, so this fits quite well with Alec and Davie.
56	'I keep goin back . . . God knows.'	Notice that Alec here says almost the same thing as he said on page 47. Whatever he feels he's lost, it is obviously still on his mind.
57	'Ma auld hymnbook'	The fact that Alec is prepared to burn or throw out his old hymnbook shows he's put his religious phase far behind him.
58	'Ah used to think it was the *actual* sea ye could hear.'	The way Alec speaks here is a strong contrast to the vivid imagination he had when he was a young child.
58	'That bookie's done awright for himself.'	Over the few years covered in this play betting has been made legal. Even the dodgy bookie has had more success over the last few years than Davie.
59	'Listen to this. The British Working Man.'	**TASK TIME** Once you've read this page do the task called *The British Working Man* which you'll find on page 84.
61	'Bring me my bow of burning gold.'	Davie again shows his learning by quoting William Blake's poem 'Jerusalem', now often sung by English rugby supporters. **Q26** What other talent of Davie's do we find out about on this page? If he used this skill, how would his life be different?

→

Page	Quotation	Notes
61	'Reserved occupation'	A reserved occupation was a job so important that someone who did it could not be called up to the army during the war. Davie's old job, once so highly respected, now doesn't exist at all.

TASK TIME Once you've read right to the end of the play, go to page 86 and do the task you'll find there called *The End of the Play.*

Task 1

Comparing Two Versions

In the first two pages of the play we see Alec and Davie dealing with the death of Alec's mother. A few years before he wrote *Sailmaker* Alan Spence wrote a short story called 'Blue'.

Read the extract from 'Blue' below. It covers the same events as the start of the play.

My mother was ill, but that was nothing unusual. She had been ill as long as I could remember and the last few years she had been in and out of hospital. She had asthma and bronchitis and found it difficult to breathe. She had been in bed now for two or three days . . . She looked paler than I had ever seen her. My father went out to phone the doctor.

. . . By the time the doctor came my mother was much worse. He said she should go to hospital and he sent for an ambulance. When it arrived I was sent next door to Mrs. Dolan's, to wait. My father went with my mother. I watched her being carried downstairs in a stretcher. That was the last time I ever saw her.

My father came back much later and we went to bed. In the middle of the night a policeman came to the door and my father went again to the hospital. This time he came back and told me my mother was dead.

It was as if part of me already knew and accepted, but part of me cried out and denied it. I cried into my pillow and a numbness came on me, shielding me from the real pain. I was lying there, sobbing, but the other part of me, the part that accepted, simply looked on. I was watching myself crying, watching my puny grief from somewhere else. I was me and I was not-me . . .

Out on the landing I opened the stairhead window and looked out across the back courts. The breeze was warm. Everything was very ordinary. Nothing had changed. The sun shone on the grey brick tenement buildings, on the railings

→

and the tumbledown walls and middens, on the dustbins and the spilled ashes. It glinted on windows and on bits of broken glass. It was like something I remembered, something from a dream. Across the back a tiny boy was standing, quite still, blowing on a mouth organ, playing the same two notes over and over again . . .

On the morning of the funeral we were getting the house ready for the people who would be there afterwards. My father was up on a chair, washing the windows. I was raking out the ashes from the fireplace . . .

I turned to look at my father. He was stepping down from the chair but he didn't look where he was putting his feet and he stepped right into the bucket of water he'd been using, soaking himself and splashing it all over the floor. It was like something from a film. The laughter swelled and burst out of me. I couldn't contain it. It took control. I laughed till I cried, and through the tears I saw that my father was laughing too.

It was after the funeral and we'd all come back in taxis. Somehow I was standing apart, on my own, across the road from our close . . . Again I had the feeling of watching myself. I looked across at the building. Home. Soon everything would be back to normal and nobody would notice that everything had changed.

I don't know what I had expected. A sign. Jesus to come walking out of the close and tell me everything was all right. A window in the sky to open and God to lean out and say my mother had arrived safe.

I looked up at the sky, trying to lose myself in the shifting of the clouds. I focused on the shapes, willing them to change into something I could grasp. I half closed my eyes. I could almost see a cross . . .

After everybody had gone, my father sat for a long time looking into the fire. Outside it was growing dark. I closed the curtains, shutting out the night, drawing in the room about us.

→

> The table was littered with plates, cups, an ashtray, spilled crumbs. My father said we could clear it all up in the morning. I felt as if the day had gone on forever.
>
> 'Aye,' said my father, turning to me. 'In the morning.'

Now answer these questions. It might help if you work with a partner. If you each have a copy of this book, one of you can have it open at these pages and one of you can open the book at the first two pages of the play script.

First, look for the **similarities** between the two versions:

1 Which details appear in both texts?

2 Note down any words or phrases that appear in both texts.

Now look for the **differences** between the texts:

3 Are there any details in the play script that aren't in the story version?

4 Are there any details in the story version that aren't in the play script?

Now **evaluate** what Spence has done:

5 What can Spence achieve with the play script that he can't do with the story version of this material?

6 What can Spence achieve in the short story that he can't do with the play script version of this material?

7 Which version do you prefer? Why?

Finally, **reflect** on what Spence has done.

8 Why do you think he told the same story twice in different ways?

Once you've answered all the questions, turn your book upside down to read what Alan Spence said about this part of the play.

There's always things in your life that you're dealing with for your whole life, in my case very obviously my mother dying when I was so young. I was eleven when my mother died and it was a huge traumatic experience for me. I think something like that sets you questioning the whole meaning of existence. The reality of having someone as close as your mother taken from you sets all those big questions into play in your mind.

Task 2

Music in the Play

Characters in the play often mention music, or sing songs. Alan Spence, who wrote the play, says:

> I've been aware of music since I was very young. The radio was always on in our house and growing up through the '60s the music was hugely important to me.

> Music is a good way of suggesting very profound emotions. For most people those emotions are expressed in popular song. Music has resonance. It suggests other levels of meaning.

> Music also gave me a way of pinning something to a time. You just hear the opening bars of My Generation and it's 1965. You're there.

You will understand the atmosphere of the play much better if you can listen to some of the music at the right point in the script. You can download all the music easily and legally from a website such as iTunes, or put together a Spotify playlist.

If you can find the versions listed below, then you will be listening to the music exactly as it sounds to the characters in the play. These songs are the pop music of the time in which the play is set.

Page	Song Title	Version By
9	Red Sails in the Sunset	Fats Domino
11	Last Train to San Fernando	Johnny Duncan and the Bluegrass Boys
13	Singing the Blues	Tommy Steele
47	My Generation	The Who
51, 52	Where the Blue of the Night Meets the Gold of the Day	Bing Crosby
55	Honky Tonk Angels	Buddy Holly

The last four songs are a little different. The Sash My Father Wore is a sectarian song, often sung by members of the Protestant group known as the Orange Order. Give Me Oil in My Lamp and Will Your Anchor Hold are hymns. The versions suggested below will let you hear the words.

In the case of *Will Your Anchor Hold* these words have extra meaning if you remember that Davie used to work in the shipbuilding industry. However, the version by Robin Mark is a bit slow – this hymn should really be sung much more quickly, with real vigour, and sound quite stirring. *Clementine* is a traditional American song.

Page	Song Title	Version By
28	*The Sash My Father Wore*	The Broadsiders
33	*Give Me Oil In My Lamp*	The Christian Choristers
34	*Will Your Anchor Hold*	Staithes Fishermen's Choir
39	*Clementine*	Paul Austin Kelly

On page 55, Alec angrily says to Davie that they are 'livin like bloody Steptoe an Son!' This was a very popular 1960s TV sitcom about a father and son who ran a scrapyard together. The son, Harold, was always trying to improve himself or get away to a better life, but never quite managed, and always felt that his father Albert held him back. There are lots of clips, and entire episodes, of this on YouTube. Watching some of these would help you understand how Alec feels at this stage in the play.

Task 3

Group Discussion

To pass the Creation and Production Unit in National 5, you have to demonstrate your talking skills in at least one **spoken interaction**. One way that you could do this is by taking part in a group discussion on *Sailmaker* as you work through the play.

Your teacher will watch, or perhaps record, your discussion, and will be looking for the following skills.

- What you say should be clearly **understandable at first hearing**.
- You should choose the right sort of **language** and vocabulary.
- Your meaning will also come across though your use of **non-verbal communication** – your eye contact, gestures, facial expression and body language.
- You must choose the right **ideas and content** to use.
- Throughout the discussion, you should use **detailed language**.
- The discussion should be **of some length** so your teacher sees you demonstrate all these skills.

Before taking part in this group discussion task you need to read a particular section of the play.

Start near the bottom of page 36 when Alec begins his very long speech. Read up to when Davie calls Alec a 'wee bugger' in the middle of page 39 and starts to hit him. You should notice that in most of this extract Alec is speaking and explaining directly to us, the audience.

Once you've read this part of the play, get into a group.

It's a good idea not to have more than four people in your group. That way everyone will have a chance to speak. Your teacher might ask someone to lead the discussion. One person in your group should be ready to explain your answers to the rest of the class afterwards.

In your discussion you should try to get the fullest possible answer for each question. Sometimes a question might have more than one possible answer.

In your group, discuss these questions:

1 Why do you think Alec feels the need to go to the Mission?
2 Look closely at the second paragraph of Alec's long speech.

('Ah cut across . . . out into the street.') What does this paragraph tell you about his environment? Do you think that has any influence in his religious behaviour?

3 Why do you think Alec feels so awkward when he is introduced to the African visitors?

4 Why do you think Alec finds Mrs Lutula's question so difficult to answer?

5 Alec can't answer Mrs Lutula's question. He runs away from the Mission and never goes back. What does that tell us about his religious faith?

6 Why do you think Alec is so angry with Davie when he gets home?

7 Look at how Alec speaks to his father on pages 38 and 39. What does this tell us about the age and stage that he's reached? What does it tell us about his relationship with his father?

8 Why is it important that the word 'auld' is used three times near the bottom of page 38 and the top of page 39?

9 What makes Davie end up so angry that he hits his own son?

Task 4

The British Working Man

On pages 59 and 60 of *Sailmaker*, Davie and Alec find a book called *Peoples of the World* and read a chapter called *The British Working Man*. They are very sarcastic about what they read here. The book sounds factual, but not much in it actually matches Davie's experience of life.

On the left you will find quotations from the book they read. Copy them into your jotter. On the right, write in details of the same aspect of Davie's life. You may reflect on the whole play, but think especially about how Davie ends up. The first has been done for you.

The book they find	**Davie's life**
'His housing conditions were once poor but have been greatly improved.'	*Davie's living conditions are now so bad he has to burn his possessions for warmth.*
'He is perhaps at his best in skilled individual occupations as, for example, in the many aspects of shipbuilding.'	
'He works without rush but consistently.'	
'He will follow the fortunes of his local [football] team with great enthusiasm.'	
'His summer interest in cricket will not be so emotional, but is often deep.'	

The book they find   Davie's life

'Better housing,
old age pensions,
security of employment –
on these he is now
seeing practical results.'

'Many men seek for
their sons better
opportunities than they
had in their youth.'

'The other man's job so
frequently appears more
attractive than one's
own.'

'In theory an astute
bookmaker should be
able to make his book
so that he cannot lose.'

Task 5

The End of the Play

At the end of the play Alec and Davie's situation is so desperate that they are burning furniture and possessions just to keep warm. The end of the play is only the start of more changes for them.

Davie says that they're about to 'get rehoused', and that this will be a 'fresh start' for them. In the 1960s and 1970s many old flats and houses in Glasgow were demolished. The residents were often moved to new high rise blocks. Many of these blocks soon turned out to have their own terrible problems. We might wonder whether their 'fresh start' will bring them more difficulties.

Re-read pages 61–62 carefully.

Lots of things that matter to Davie come to an end on this page. We can also see on this page that he realises and accepts that some important parts of his life have ended.

How do we see the end here of:

Davie's family life

Davie's career

Davie's home

Davie's marriage?

Now re-read pages 63 and 64 carefully.

We find out that Davie never did mend the yacht for Alec. What does this tell us about Davie?

Read Alec's last long speech and answer these questions:

What do you think that the burning of the yacht stands for or symbolises? (You might find more than one answer.)

Why do you think Spence gets Alec to mention the dead Viking chief?

Now think about the way the play ends, keeping the whole play in mind as you do so:

Do you think the ending is sad or happy? Why?

Do you think the ending is optimistic or pessimistic? Why?

Finally, think about all four characters in the play.

For each one, write a short paragraph to explain what you think might happen to them in the next ten years after the play ends. You should have more to say about Alec and Davie than about Ian and Billy, because they are more important characters.

Now turn the book upside down. Read what Alan Spence said about what really happened to him and his dad after the part of their lives which he covered in the play.

I went to Glasgow Uni in 1966 to study law, which I did for two years. It was about getting on, getting a job. I just blundered into law without any notion of whether it was suitable. Later I switched to an arts degree, then dropped out and went travelling. I came back in 1974 to finish a degree. By that time I knew that writing was the most important thing.

My dad and I were rehoused in 1968. Our tenement was demolished and we were moved to a new high rise flat.

My dad lost it a wee bit towards the end of his life and maybe was hitting the bottle a bit. I managed to find him a bedsit with a young family involved in the local Baptist church. His life was transformed. He found a focus and peace at the church and became a well-loved character in the congregation until he died in 1979. He was 63.

Task 6

The Structure of the Play

Some plays are very long, some much shorter. Some plays (such as those by Shakespeare) are divided into many short scenes, while *Sailmaker* just has two named scenes.

Despite these differences, most plays share a very similar structure. We can describe this structure in four stages, which usually go in the following order:

1 **Exposition:** In this section the main characters and the basic situation of the play are introduced to us.

2 **Turning point:** Something very important happens to change the way the play is going, or the main character comes to an important decision or realisation.

3 **Climax:** At this point the action and emotions of the play come to a head. This is the most exciting or dramatic point of the play. It is usually near, but not at, the end.

4 **Resolution:** This follows on from the climax. Events and emotions are finally dealt with and the play feels finished off.

Start by working alone or with a partner. Decide what the exposition, turning point, climax and resolution of *Sailmaker* are. Share your answers with the rest of the class to make sure that you all agree. Then write two or three sentences to explain what happens in each of these four sections.

Next, answer these questions:

1 How does Alan Spence, who wrote *Sailmaker*, create impact at the turning point of the play?

2 How does Spence create impact at the climax?

Task 7

Characters

Once you have read the whole play you can take an overview of all the characters.

If you are working alone, build up a grid for each character like the one below. Fill in as many details as you can in each quadrant. If you are working in a group, tackle just one character. Present your work as a poster. You could put a picture in the middle as well as the character's name.

What happens to him
in the play

How he changes during
the play

Name

Reasons to like or admire
this character

Reasons to dislike or challenge
this character

Task 8

Themes in *Sailmaker*

A theme is something the writer wants you to think about or learn about as you read a text. Themes are big ideas. You can usually say a theme in just one or two words. Love, hate and war are all themes that many writers have used.

This play has a number of themes. You will find a list of them below. Your task is to prove that Alan Spence is dealing with these themes in the play.

Choose a theme and put it in the centre of a new page in your jotter. Draw lines out from the centre and write down details and examples from the play to prove that Spence is examining that theme.

There are eight themes on the list. If you share these themes out around the class you should be able to cover them all. You could present your findings as a PowerPoint or poster for other members of the class to look at and copy.

The themes

Grief and loss

Religion

Family life

Poverty

Violence

Dreams and ambitions

Social class differences

Escapism/imagination

What your page might look like

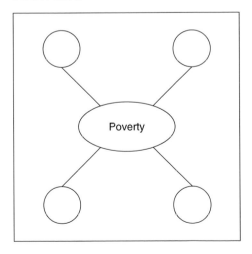

Task 9

Contrasts

Alan Spence often uses contrast in this play. That is, he puts two things side by side to let us see how they are different. This lets him explore his ideas and themes.

- Sometimes he contrasts two people within a family:
  e.g. contrasting Alec with Davie.

- Sometimes he contrasts familes: e.g. showing us how Alec and Davie are different from Ian and Billy.

- Sometimes he contrasts two moods: e.g. following a sad scene with a more humorous one.

- Sometimes he makes a contrast in subject or theme, so a scene about children playing could be followed by one that is about more serious or adult problems.

This is a good task to do for revision before your National 5 exam. The play has been divided into numbered sections. After you have read each section, decide and note down how it contrasts with the previous section. The first answer has been done for you as an example. (By the way, if you are studying this play to write about it in an exam, this is a good task to do for revision.)

1 First read section 1 from page 6: 'Sometimes I wake up' to page 8: 'In the mornin'.

2 Now read section 2 from page 8: 'Ah had a yacht' to page 15: 'Don't forget the comics'.

   Q How does section 2 contrast with the previous section?

   A *The previous scene was a sad one about Alec's mother dying. This is a happy one.*

3 Now read section 3 from page 16: 'Marlinspikes' to page 17: 'Mainsail'. How does section 3 contrast with the previous section?

4 Now read section 4 from page 18: 'A wee game' to page 19: 'Shove ye in the pool' and explain how this contrasts with the previous section.

5 Now read section 5 from page 19: 'Eh Billy' to page 22: 'If ah ever dae' and explain how this contrasts with the previous section.

6 Now read section 6 from page 22: 'How ye doin wee yin?' to page 23: 'See you later' and explain how this contrasts with the previous section.

7 Now read section 7 from page 23: 'Ah've got the string' to page 25: 'C'mon, we'll go huntin' and explain how this contrasts with the previous section.

8 Now read section 8 from 'Hey Davie' on page 25 to page 29: 'A Protestant!' and explain how this contrasts with the previous section.

9 Now read section 9 from page 30: 'C'mon, ah'll be Alan Morton' to page 31: 'Or a tick man' and explain how this contrasts with the previous section.

10 Now read section 10 from page 31: 'What's up wi your face?' to the end of the act on page 32 and explain how this contrasts with the previous section.

11 Now read section 11 from the start of Act Two on page 33 to page 38: '. . .back so early' and explain how this contrasts with the previous section.

12 Now read section 12 from page 38: 'What's the matter?' to page 41: 'Wallop' and explain how this contrasts with the previous section.

13 Now read section 13 from page 41: 'How was the exam?' to page 45: 'Ready or not' and explain how this contrasts with the previous section.

14 Now read section 14 from page 45: 'Factory's shuttin doon' to page 48: 'Candlelight dinner for two sir?' and explain how this contrasts with the previous section.

15 Now read section 15 from page 48: 'Hey Michelangelo' to page 51: 'What can ye dae?' and explain how this contrasts with the previous section.

16 Now read section 16 from page 51: 'Where the blue of the night' to 'Wallop' at the bottom of page 55 and explain how this contrasts with the previous section.

17 Now read section 17 from the top of page 56 to the end of the play and explain how this contrasts with the previous section.

If you have been using this task for revision you can also use the 17 sections to help you revise in other ways. You could find and learn a useful quotation from each section. You could also decide which theme(s) Spence is tackling in each section and back this up with evidence from that part of the play.

The Scottish Set Text Questions

One of your National 5 exams is called Critical Reading. This exam is 90 minutes long and will ask you to do two things.

In Part 2 you will write a critical essay about a text you have studied in class. You might choose to write about *Sailmaker* there, and we will cover that later in this book.

In Part 1 of this exam you will answer questions on a set Scottish text. You will read an extract from *Sailmaker*, which will be printed in the exam paper. This will be followed by four or five questions.

- The first few questions will be about the extract itself. These questions will be worth 2, 3 or 4 marks. They will test your ability to understand and summarise the ideas and events in the text, and to analyse the writer's style and techniques.

- The last question will be worth 8 marks and will get you to put the extract in context, relating it to the wider play as a whole.

Part 2 is worth 20 marks in total.

Try this practice task:

First, read the section of the play that starts with Davie asking, '*What's the matter?*' about half way down page 38 and goes on to Alec saying, '*Never have tae take ma jacket off!*' about a third of the way down page 40. Alec has just come home after running away from the Mission.

Then answer these questions:

1 Summarise the key points of this exchange between Alec and Davie. Make at least 4 key points. **(4)**

2 What does Alec's language from '*Yes and here we go*' to '*maulicated Benny Lunch's granny*' tell us about his relationship with his father at this point in the play? **(4)**

3 What do the stage directions from **DAVIE**: *Oh ho! Fightin talk!* to (*Rains down a flurry of blows, just short of Alec's face*) tell us about
   a) How Alec feels about Davie? **(2)**
   b) How Davie feels about Alec? **(2)**

4 At the end of the extract, the characters discuss the exam Alec is about to take. With close reference to the rest of *Sailmaker*, explain how the theme of education is explored throughout the play. **(8)**

Critical Essay Questions

One of your National 5 exams is called Critical Reading. This exam is 90 minutes long and will ask you to do two things.

In Part 1 you will answer questions on a set Scottish text. As we have already discussed, you may choose to answer questions on *Sailmaker* there.

In Part 2 you will be asked to write a critical essay about a text you have studied in class. This is another place where you may choose to write about *Sailmaker*.

WARNING! What you **absolutely cannot do** is write about *Sailmaker* both in your critical essay **and** in the set Scottish text section of the exam. You **must** make sure you write about **different texts** in each section, and these must be from **different genres**. Your teacher will keep reminding you about this very important detail.

On the exam paper you will see the heading **PART A – DRAMA**. Under the heading you will see a box containing this wording:

> *Answers to questions in this part should refer to the text and to such relevant features as characterisation, key scene(s), structure, climax, theme, plot, conflict, setting . . .*

Then you will see two essay questions. They will not name *Sailmaker* (or any other play) but instead will be quite broad, general questions. It's up to you to recognise and choose a suitable question for the texts you have studied.

Here are some example questions that would be suitable for *Sailmaker*:

1 Choose a play which portrays a strong relationship between two of the main characters.

   Describe the nature of the relationship and, by referring to appropriate techniques, explain how the relationship influences the fate of the two characters concerned.

2 Choose a play in which one of the characters achieves his or her aim or ambition.

   State what the character's aim or ambition is and, by referring to appropriate techniques, go on to identify what aspects of his or her personality help him or her to overcome the obstacles in the way of success.

3 Choose a play which you feel has a turning point.

Describe briefly what happens at this turning point and then, by referring to appropriate techniques, go on to explain how it makes an impact on the play as a whole.

4 Choose a play in which the playwright presents a flawed character who you feel is more worthy of our sympathy than criticism.

By referring to appropriate techniques, show how the character's flawed nature is revealed, then explain how, despite this, we are led to feel sympathy for her/him.

5 Choose a play which has a sad or tragic ending.

By referring to appropriate techniques, show how the ending of the play results from the strengths and/or weaknesses of the main character(s).

6 Choose a play in which there is a highly emotional scene.

By referring to appropriate techniques, show how the scene increases your understanding of the characters involved and how it is important to the unfolding of the plot of the play.

7 Choose a play in which there is a character who suffers from a human weakness such as ambition, selfishness, lack of self-knowledge, jealousy, pride or any other human weakness.

By referring to appropriate techniques, show how the weakness is revealed, then explain how this weakness affects both the characters and the events of the play.

The Writing Portfolio

For those studying National 5 English, as part of your assessment you will send away a Portfolio of two pieces of writing. These pieces must come from two different genres.

The first piece should be **creative**, which means:

- a personal or reflective essay
- a piece of prose: e.g. a short story or an extract from a novel
- a poem or a set of linked poems
- a drama script.

There are many ways in which *Sailmaker* might inspire you to write this kind of piece for your Portfolio.

You might write a **personal reflective essay** inspired by something that happens to one of the characters in the play. For example:

- You could write about a time when you were in conflict with one or both of your parents, showing how the conflict arose and how it was resolved.
- You could write about a time when you lost someone or something that really mattered to you.
- You could write about a time when you experienced personal success and achievement, reflecting on how that success changed or affected you.

You might write a **fictional story** inspired by something that happens to one of the characters in the play. For example:

- You could write a short story in which a teenager comes into conflict with one or both parents.
- You could write a short story in which a new environment or an unusual experience leads to big changes in your main character.

The second Portfolio piece should be **discursive**, which means:

- a piece of transactional writing
- a persuasive essay
- an argumentative essay
- a report.

There are many ways in which *Sailmaker* might inspire you to write this kind of piece for your Portfolio.

You might write a **two-sided argumentative essay** inspired by the play. In this kind of essay you would look at points from both sides of the argument before summing up and finally giving your own opinion. For example:

- Should boxing be banned?
- Is private education a good thing or a bad thing?
- Is following a football team just an excuse for tribal violence or can it have a positive effect on fans?
- Has gambling become too easy and should it now be restricted?

You might write a **one-sided persuasive essay** inspired by the play. In this kind of essay you would have a clear point that you believe in, and would spend the whole essay giving evidence and examples to try to convince the reader. In this case your essay title would be worded as a strong statement of what you believe. For example:

- Boxing is bloodthirsty and should be banned.
- State school education is just as good as private education.
- Following a football team is just an excuse for tribal violence.
- Gambling has become too easy and should be restricted.

Whatever you write, you will need to plan first. If you choose to write an argumentative or persuasive essay you will also need to spend time on research. After you have written a first version of your piece your teacher will read it and give you advice about how you can redraft it to improve it.